WRITERS AND THEIR WORK

ISOBEL ARMSTRONG
General Editor

FRANZ KAFKA

FRANZ KAFKA

A photograph of young Kafka with a sheep. Reproduced from the Kafka archive by courtesy of Archiv Klaus Wagenbach, Berlin.

FRANZ KAFKA

Michael Wood

NORTHCOTE

BRITISH COUNCIL

ATLANTIC
PUBLISHERS & DISTRIBUTORS (P) LTD

This edition is published by

ATLANTIC

PUBLISHERS & DISTRIBUTORS (P) LTD

7/22, Ansari Road, Darya Ganj, New Delhi-110 002
Tel: 40775252, 23273880, 23275880, 23280451; Fax: +91-11-23285873
E-mail: orders@atlanticbooks.com; Web: www.atlanticbooks.com

By arrangement with
Northcote House Publishers Ltd
Horndon House, Horndon, Tavistock, Devon, PL19 9NQ,
United Kingdom. (T)+44(0)1822 810066; (F)+44(0)1822 810034
(E) northcote.house@virgin.net and (W) www.northcotehouse.co.uk
The *Writers and their Work* series is published in association with the British Council.

First Indian Reprint 2010
First published in 2003 by Northcote House Publishers Ltd

ISBN 978-81-269-1285-8

For Sale in the Indian sub-continent only. Not for export elsewhere.

British Library Cataloguing-in-Publication Data
A catalogue record for this book is available from the British Library

Typeset by TW Typesetting, Plymouth, Devon
Printed in India at Nice Printing Press, A-33/3A, Site-IV,
Industrial Area, Sahibabad, Ghaziabad, U.P.

Contents

Biographical Outline

1883	Franz Kafka born 3 July in Prague, to Hermann Kafka and Julie Kafka née Löwy. His two brothers Georg and Heinrich die very young. His sisters Elli, Valli, and Ottla are born 1889, 1890, 1892.
1893–1901	Attends German gymnasium in Prague.
1901–6	Studies German literature, then law, at German University in Prague, and at the University of Munich.
1904–5	Writes the story 'Description of a Struggle'.
1906	Works in the law office of Dr Richard Löwy. Completes doctorate in law at German University.
1907–8	Position in the Prague office of Assicurazioni Generali, an Italian insurance company. Writes the story 'Wedding Preparations in the Country'.
1908–22	Employed by the Workers' Accident Insurance Institute.
1910	Travels to Paris and Berlin.
1911	Travels to Zurich, Lugano, Milan, Paris. Spell in a sanatorium at Erlenbach near Zurich. Starts writing the novel *Amerika*.
1912	Sanatorium in the Hartz Mountains. Meets Felice Bauer in Prague. Finishes the volume of stories called *Contemplation*. Writes the stories 'The Judgement', 'The Stoker' (first chapter of *Amerika*), and 'The Metamorphosis'.
1913	*Contemplation* published. Visits Felice in Berlin. 'The Judgement' and 'The Stoker' published. Travels to Vienna, Venice, and Riva. Meets Grete Bloch, Felice's friend.

1914 Engaged to Felice Bauer. Early work on *The Castle* Work on *The Trial*. Writes 'In the Penal Colony'. Breaks off the engagement with Felice.

1915 Work on *The Trial*. 'The Stoker' wins Theodor Fontane Prize. 'The Metamorphosis' published.

1916 Writes some of the stories that will appear in the volume *A Country Doctor*.

1917 Renews the engagement with Felice. More work on *Country Doctor* stories. Writes and rewrites most of the parables and epigrams now usually known as his 'Aphorisms'. Tuberculosis diagnosed. Breaks off engagement again.

1918 Continues to work on the 'Aphorisms'. Writes 'The Great Wall of China'.

1919 Brief engagement to Julie Wohryzek. 'In the Penal Colony' and *A Country Doctor* published. Writes 'Letter to his Father'.

1920 Meets Milena Jesenska in Vienna. Works on the stories that will appear in the volume *A Hunger Artist*.

1921 Sanatorium in the Tatra Mountains.

1922 Works on *The Castle*. Last meeting with Milena. Writes 'A Hunger Artist', and 'Investigations of a Dog'.

1923 Meets Dora Dymant. Moves to Berlin. Writes the stories 'The Burrow' and 'Josephine the Singer'.

1924 Dies 3 June in Kierling near Vienna. *A Hunger Artist* published.

1925 *The Trial* published.

1926 *The Castle* published.

1927 *Amerika* published.

Abbreviations

B. *Briefe an Milena* (Frankfurt: Fischer, 1986).

C. *The Castle*, trans. Willa and Edwin Muir (New York: Schocken, 1995).

CS *The Complete Stories*, ed. Nahum N. Glatzer (New York: Schocken, 1971).

D. *Diaries 1910–1923*, trans. Joseph Kresh and Martin Greenberg (London: Penguin, 1982).

G. *The Great Wall of China and Other Short Works*, trans. and ed. Malcolm Pasley (London: Penguin, 1991).

H. *Hochzeitsvorbereitungen auf dem Lande und andere Prosa aus dem Nachlaß* (Frankfurt: Fischer, 1983).

M. *Metamorphosis and Other Stories*, trans. and ed. Malcolm Pasley (London: Penguin, 1992).

P. *Der Proceß* (Frankfurt: Fischer, 1993).

S. *Das Schloß* (Frankfurt: Fischer, 1994).

SE *Sämtliche Erzählungen* (Frankfurt: Fischer, 1970).

T. *Tagebücher 1910–1923* (Frankfurt: Fischer, 1973).

TR. *The Trial*, trans. Willa and Edwin Muir (New York: Schocken, 1995).

I have adapted the English translations very slightly on a few occasions, in order to bring the language closer to the structure of the German sentences.

1

A Common Confusion

In the months to come
It rang on like the burden of his freedom
To try for the right tone – not tract, not thesis –
And walk away from floggings.

(Seamus Heaney, 'Chekhov on Sakhalin')

There is a very short story by Kafka, a desperate parable, called 'A Common Confusion', written in October 1917. The title was given to the piece by Kafka's friend and editor Max Brod, but the words themselves appear in the story's stark and (in German) verbless opening sentence: 'A common occurrence, resulting in a common confusion' (*SE* 303–4; *CS* 429–30). We may want to translate a little more literally to catch the force of the phrasing. 'An everyday [*alltäglich*] occurrence: putting up with it [*sein Ertragen*] an everyday confusion.' What is the event announced in this way?

A visits B to have a preliminary talk with him about an important piece of business they are engaged in. The journey takes ten minutes each way. The next day, when the business is to be concluded, the same journey takes A ten hours one way, although everything else about the trip seems to him unchanged. A learns that B, irritated by A's delay, has just left for A's village. A is advised to stay and wait, but rushes back home. This time he completes the journey, perhaps because he is not thinking of it, in a moment – 'geradezu in einem Augenblick'. At home he learns that B had arrived early, just after A had left – indeed the two men had met at the door, B had reminded A of their business, but A had said he had no time now, he had to hurry off. Fortunately, and in spite of everything, B is still waiting for A in his room, so A will now be able to explain. He rushes up the stairs happily, but stumbles near the top, twists a muscle, and, 'almost fainting with the pain, incapable even of uttering a cry, only able to moan faintly in the darkness, he hears B – impossible to tell whether at a great distance or quite near him – stamping down the stairs in a violent rage and vanishing for good'. The story ends there, its only editorial comments the opening sentence and a remark in the middle about A's 'incomprehensible behaviour' – and even this remark could be taken as a voicing of B's view of his elusive partner.

There are many things to be said about this story, notably about the weirdly shifting grounds of the failed second encounter, as if failure were an absolute, and mere empirical reality had to shape up to its orders, and about the enormous anxiety Kafka is able to generate around these entirely algebraic figures and their unspecified bit of business. But here I want only to comment on the function of the first sentence, and to offer it as a modest introduction to the intimate texture of Kafka's work. Can this sort of thing really be an everyday occurrence?

Of course we do not have to be too literal about the word 'everyday', which even in English does not mean every day. Nevertheless, the story is too unsettling to conform to its mild discursive promise. It is not that we are suspended in ambiguity: this occurrence both is and is not an everyday one, the everyday both does and does not look like this. These statements are true but only restate our hesitation as if we were not hesitating. In the actual practice of reading we have to work harder, to follow out interpretative decisions we may not even have taken consciously. If we edge towards a sarcastic interpretation of the opening sentence – we know what the everyday is, and it does not include expanding and shrinking time or distance, or accidents perfectly timed to prevent the success of our ventures – we express our conviction that life is not like this. The move is similar to all the (thousands of) interpretations of Kafka that call his work dreamlike or nightmarish. These gestures are helpful as rough shorthand, first attempts at an evocation of Kafka's world; but also betray an alarming confidence in the rationality of waking reality, as if nightmares always knew their place, and could be guaranteed to stay in the realm of sleep.

If we go to the other end of the interpretative spectrum, and take the opening sentence as straight as we can – this sequence of events may seem strange, and may not happen every day, but such things are, alas, more ordinary than we like to believe – we seem to be colluding with a self-torturing mind that draws the universe into its need for disaster, to be treating that mind as if there were nothing damaged or estranged about it. Is there a middle ground? Perhaps, but Kafka is not inviting us to look for it or settle for it.

This, in caricatural form, is how I take the interpretative motions of this text to work. We are invited to believe that we know what the everyday is, only to be nudged almost immediately into a worry that we do not. We are then tempted perhaps to take our ignorance as a resting place, a form of negative knowledge. The everyday disappears, everything is strange. But the eerie discipline of Kafka's text, its comprehension of our insecurities, compels us to further questions. Is the story all that strange, are we going to say we recognize nothing here? Can we say, for instance, that a happy end to this story, a full reconciliation between A and B, would seem to us more everyday than the terrible terminal accident? It would certainly be more satisfying, but would it be more everyday? Quite often it is the accident that is going to seem everyday, even if we are not paranoid. We have also, come to think of it, taken plenty of ten-minute journeys that took ten hours. But now we are in danger of making the story seem more ordinary than it is, or fencing it off in some space that is safely metaphorical, and we need to start again. The sequence is endless, but not useless – far from it.

'The knowing animals are aware', Kafka's Prague compatriot Rainer Maria Rilke wrote in his first Duino Elegy, 'that we are not really at home in/our interpreted world'.[1] These wonderful lines are often taken as contrasting the (merely) interpreted world with another, more elemental world beyond interpretation. The more we think of the image, Peter and Sheila Stern say, 'the more it disquiets us by implying that where "interpretation" is at issue, there is an allusion entailed to something not interpreted, the presence of some sort of absolute text'.[2] This must be very close to Rilke's mood, but a simpler, more radical reading is also possible. The interpreted world may be distinguished not only from a uninterpreted world but from other interpretations of the same world and from the world itself as always interpreted but always resisting interpretation. Rilke would then be saying that the world just is an interpreted world, whichever way we turn it. The animals are knowing – or clever, or inventive, (*findig*) – because they need to be. Their interpretations of the world are perhaps more fundamental than ours but they are still interpretations.

'The intellectual foundation of every human society', Erich Heller suggested in *The Disinherited Mind,*

> is a generally accepted model of reality. One of the major difficulties of human existence is, I think, due to the fact that this model of reality is in every single case a mere *interpretation* of the world, and yet exerts, as long as it seems the valid interpretation, the subtly compelling claim to being accepted as the only true picture of the universe, indeed as truth itself. This difficulty, manifesting itself in the deeper strata of doubt . . . develops easily into a mental epidemic in epochs in which a certain model of reality crumbles and collapses. It seems that we have lived in such an epoch for a long time.[3]

Heller was writing in 1952, and it is hard to think of a better definition of the crisis of belief to which modernism, in its diverse forms, was a major response. Interpretation, we might say, is everyone's practice but becomes a preoccupation, an arena of difficult doubt, when old agreements fail or are exposed, when truths are seen to be dependent on interpretation, not to precede it.

In daily life our interpretative hesitations are often resolved quickly enough. But we can imagine them going on and on, and Kafka constructed a whole fictional world out of such a possibility. It is for this reason that his moral universe can seem both strange to the point of privacy and familiar to the point of despair. We scarcely know whether the work is driven by the most intense personal nightmare or by the complicated currents of the largest modern history, although we could indeed start wondering whether those apparent alternatives are real ones. Kafka was among the first to see that history has its neuroses and psychoses, and that they are strikingly similar to those of the individual. The chief suggestion of this little book is that Kafka owes his place in the literature of the twentieth century not to his ability to invent the fantastic, or to make the ordinary seem strange and the strange ordinary, but to his uncanny understanding of the strategies developed by humankind for what I shall call the taming of surprise – ways of living with what ought to be unbelievable but is not – and of the personal and historical consequences of our reliance on those strategies.

2

The Student of Prague

> I read a theological interpretation of it somewhere, he said bemused. The Father and the Son idea. The Son striving to be atoned with the Father.
>
> (James Joyce, *Ulysses*)

Franz Kafka was born in Prague in 1883, just once. Kafka the writer was born several times over, in various places and at various dates, notably in 1925 and 1926, when *The Trial* and *The Castle* were posthumously published, in Berlin and Munich respectively. But at no point do we get a more dramatic or more revealing glimpse of the emerging author than in the autumn of 1912. In the night of 22–3 September of that year, Kafka wrote his first major story, 'The Judgement'. Later that month he began his first novel, *Amerika*, interrupting himself from 17 November to 8 December in order to complete the most famous of all his fictions, 'The Metamorphosis'. If he had produced nothing apart from what he wrote in these eleven weeks, his place in literary history would be secure. He abandoned *Amerika* at the beginning of 1913, returning to it only briefly in the summer and autumn of 1914 – he also abandoned his other longer works, *The Trial* (begun in August 1914), and *The Castle* (begun in earnest in January 1922), so that he presents to us the curious figure of the great novelist who never finished a novel. This is not the most curious thing about Kafka as a writer.

While he was working on *Amerika*, in November 1912, Kafka wrote to Felice Bauer, whom he had met a little earlier in the year and who was later to become his fiancée, that the novel was 'the first longer work' in which he felt secure 'after fifteen years of comfortless torment'.[1] Torment as a writer, he means, and he is probably not exaggerating. But the time span is what is striking here. Even if fifteen years is a rounded figure, not meant to be precise, it takes us back to the 1890s, when Kafka was a schoolboy, still attending the German gymnasium in Prague, and to an earlier time than that of any of Kafka's known writings. The 29-year-old employee of the Workers' Accident Insurance Institute in Prague is saying that he has been trying and failing to write since he was 14. It is true that he is talking about 'longer work', but that is where the other dates in 1912 help us, since they allow us to see that his breakthrough in shorter fiction had already occurred, but only just.

Kafka had by that time written a number of short pieces and published some of them in magazines, and in December 1912 – what a year – eighteen of them appeared as a book called *Contemplation*, printed in Leipzig and dated 1913. This is a haunting book, and once or twice strikes a note we can now recognize as Kafka's. But the Kafka who allows us retrospectively to recognize the note is still to be born, and soon after the manuscript for *Contemplation* has been delivered comes the extraordinary night in which 'The Judgement' is written – in one stretch, Kafka says in his diary, from ten at night to six in the morning. 'Around two I looked at the clock for the last time.' He evokes 'the frightful effort and joy' he found in the development of the story, and the excitement of the discovery that 'everything can be said', that 'for every notion, even the strangest, a great fire is prepared, in which it is consumed and rises again'. He also speaks of the 'shameful abasements of writing' (*T*. 183–4; *D*. 212–13). Writing here for him is 'novel writing' (*Romanschreiben*), which in context seems to mean writing fiction rather than writing at length. Joy and shame, the consuming and delivering fire: when Kafka says his fifteen-year torment is over, he does not mean writing is now easy or unproblematic. He means only that he knows he has become a writer, rather than a person just waiting or wanting to be one. That he can interrupt *Amerika* to write 'Metamorphosis' suggests a flickering but powerful inspiration, even a compulsion, and the ability to feed more than one fire at the same time. This sense of a vocation, however shameful and strained and interruptible, will never leave him.

'Writing as a form of prayer' (*H.* 252), Kafka wrote in a late fragment, but the address of the prayer was mostly unholy.

> Writing is a sweet, wonderful reward, but for what? In the night it was evident to me with the clarity of a childhood art lesson that it is the reward for serving the Devil. This descent to the dark powers, this unchaining of spirits bound by nature, these questionable embraces and whatever else goes on down there, that one knows no more about up here, when one writes stories in the sunlight. Perhaps there is also another kind of writing, I know only this one; in the night, when fear keeps me from sleeping, I know only this one. And what's devilish about it seems very clear to me.[2]

What is devilish in writing is its vanity, its temptation to gloat over the very indirectness Kafka elsewhere complains about, a celebration of the unlived life. The writer, he says, is like a person wishing for his or her own death in order to see how the mourning will go, the persistent author of fictions that place him at the centre of an imaginary stage. 'He dies (or he does not live), and weeps for himself continuously'.

But, for Kafka, writing is irresistible. It is what he has, what he does. In 'writing and what goes with it', he tells his father (or would have told him if he had ever sent the letter in which he wrote these words), he makes 'small attempts at independence, attempts at flight', and to watch over these attempts, to see that no harm comes to them or could come to them, 'is my duty or rather my life' (*H.* 159). Even prayers to the Devil testify to the absent altars of God. 'There can be a knowledge of the diabolical, but no belief in it, for more of the diabolical than is actually present does not exist' (*H.* 39; *G.* 96). 'Our art', Kafka writes in one his most luminous fragments, 'is to be blinded by the truth: only the light on the retreating, grimacing face is true, nothing else' (*H.* 35; *G.* 89).

In the 1890s, Prague was the busy capital of the province of Bohemia, itself part of the strange entity known as Austria-Hungary, which had come into being in 1867, when the so-called Compromise, or *Ausgleich,* established the Dual Monarchy: the Kingdom of Hungary and the Austrian Empire. The double name left a lot out: what was not Hungary was by no means all Austria. What it was, the only single thing it was,

was Habsburg, the collected possessions of a dynasty, not a modern nation. The history is complicated but we can get an elementary sense of it by recalling the names of the states and regions that went into the empire: Austria, Hungary, Bohemia, Moravia, Galicia, Banat, Bosnia, Herzegovina, Slavonia, Dalmatia, Croatia, Styria, Tyrol. We may also wish to remember some of the ethnic or linguistic groupings that made up this same empire: German, Hungarian, Czech, Slovak, Polish, Romanian, Italian, Serbo-Croat, Slovene, Ruthenian.

The Austrian Robert Musil calls this place Kakanien, because of the k's echoing in the words *königlich* and *kaiserlich*, royal and imperial. Translators keep the term, I'm sure rightly, only slightly modified into Kakania, but we could get a livelier, if less dignified feel of the joke if we thought of the place as Cacophonia – along the lines of Freedonia as it appears in *Duck Soup*.

> It was liberal according to its constitution, but it was clerically governed. It was clerically governed, but people lived as freethinkers. All citizens were equal before the law, but not everyone was a citizen. There was a parliament, which made so forceful a use of its freedom that it was usually kept closed; but there was also an emergency rule, which allowed the country to do without parliament, and every time people became content with absolutism, the crown reinstated parliamentary government.[3]

A little later Musil's narrator explains what Austro-Hungarian consciousness – literally feeling for the state (*Staatsgefühl*) – is like. Any thoughtful subject of the United Kingdom of Great Britain and Northern Ireland will already know what he is talking about, and everyone can imagine these relations.

> It did not consist of an Austrian part and a Hungarian part which, as one might imagine, complemented each other. It consisted of a whole and a part, namely of a Hungarian and an Austro-Hungarian consciousness, and the second one was at home in Austria, so that the Austrian consciousness was actually without a home. The Austrian appeared only in Hungary, and there only as someone disliked; at home he called himself a member of all the kingdoms and provinces represented in the parliament of the Austro-Hungarian monarchy, which meant he was an Austrian plus a Hungarian minus that same Hungarian . . . It was for this reason that many people simply called themselves Czechs, Poles, Slovenes or Germans.[4]

Musil adds that the secrets of the Dualism (a technical term for the Dual Monarchy, he says) were at least as hard to penetrate as those of the Trinity.

Kafka was not an Austro-Hungarian in this sense, he was a German, as was Rilke, in spite of the fact that a country called Germany had recently been unified without them. Even in the late 1930s many German speakers still pictured themselves as part of a single transnational culture. We may think of Karl Rossmann, in *Amerika*, introducing himself as a German 'from Prague in Bohemia'. But, of course, the Germans were a minority in the largely Czech Bohemia, and the Jews were only a part of that minority. And if many people 'simply' called themselves Czechs or Germans, Kafka belonged to a group that called itself both, and called itself Jewish as well.

This variously determined (and variously experienced) identity is important, and it cannot be an accident that so many of the figures we associate with artistic and intellectual modernity came from this rickety empire. Apart from Kafka and Rilke and Musil, there are Freud, Wittgenstein, Broch, Mahler, Richard Strauss, Schönberg, Berg, Janáček, Klimt, and Kokoschka. 'This grotesque Austria', Musil says in his *Diaries*, 'is nothing but a particularly clear-cut case of the modern world'.[5] A clear-cut case of delusion, he means, where a kind of terminal modernity is both denied and suffered. In 1913, when Musil's great unfinished novel *The Man without Qualities* is set, the Dual Monarchy is planning a great celebration for 1918. No one in the novel knows war is coming, and with it the demise of the Austro-Hungarian Empire itself. And yet the text itself discreetly refers to what was to happen, and speaks of the empire in the past tense, 'Kakania, this now fallen, misunderstood state'.[6]

Kafka too, who was born in Prague not too long after the *Ausgleich* and died near Vienna six years after the end of the empire, wrote quite a bit about Kakania, although he usually called it China, a common metaphor in those days for any European state in its despotic, hieratic, arbitrary, slow-moving mode, but especially for Austria-Hungary, in its intricate and almost unimaginable spread. At times Kafka seems to have thought, hyperbolically, that this metaphorical China reached almost as far as China itself. In a letter to his friend Milena Jesenska, Kafka said he was reading 'a book about Tibet'. 'At the description of a settlement in the mountains on the Tibetan border I suddenly become distressed, because the village seems so desolate and neglected, so far from Vienna. At the same time I decide it's stupid to imagine Tibet is far from Vienna. How could it be far?' (*B.* 35).

The main implication, I take it, is that Tibet is neither near nor far but something else; but Kafka is also giving voice to the tempting (but stupid) thought that Tibet is just a particularly desolate and far-flung outpost of the Austro-Hungarian Empire. Vienna is also where Milena is at this moment, and there are other than imperial matters here, of course. But empire always means distance in Kafka; and distance means weakness. Yet weakness is paradoxically a form of strength, since nothing grips the mind like an absent or dead or even non-existent emperor-god. How far was Prague from Vienna? How could it be far? How could it not be far?

Much of Kafka's thinking on this subject is beautifully summarized, although distinctly over-condensed, in this fragment:

> A man doubted that the emperor was descended from the gods; he asserted that the emperor was our rightful sovereign, he did not doubt the emperor's divine mission (that was evident to him), it was only the divine descent that he doubted. This, naturally, did not cause much of a stir; when the surf flings a drop of water on to the land, that does not interfere with the eternal rolling of the sea, on the contrary, it is caused by it. (*H.* 236)

The doubting man may be registering an important theological and political difference whose importance is not recognized, does not 'cause much of a stir'. He may be making a distinction that is logically tenable but cannot matter in any other sense. And he may just be misunderstanding a metaphor – much theology is such a practice. But in all cases he is caught up in the imperial fiction: a drop in the ocean. More precisely, a drop out of the ocean, but still part of the ocean's activities. You cannot drop out of the ocean – another way of asking whether Tibet is really far from Vienna for an Austro-Hungarian subject. And the really interesting further question, perhaps, is not whether the rolling of the sea is eternal – it is not, if the sea is an empire – but why we cannot imagine it as other than eternal.

And Prague itself, 'magic Prague', as the title of Angelo Maria Ripellino's rapturous book calls it?[7] Its castle, river, ancient streets, many churches, Jewish cemetery, its largely razed ghetto. Home of *The Golem* and a whole Expressionist movie in its own right. It is easy to exaggerate the power of this place over an artist's mind; but easy also to lose the person in the place. Anything or anyone could disappear there, Kafka suggests in a note: 'Prague. Religions get lost like people' (*H.* 96).

If we do not see Kafka as the perpetually haunted student of Prague, trapped in a historical city we have completely overlaid with spooky images from his own writing, how do we see him? From all the biographies, and thinking now only of Kafka's relation to the city, several contradictory images appear. Kafka is more at home in the city than he is in himself. He likes to walk, go swimming, take a boat on the river. He loves the old and narrow streets near the castle. He attends lectures, he reads his stories to literary groups, he goes to the theatre and the cinema. He lives at home, endlessly fighting for space and quiet; he lives alone; he lives with one of his sisters. Tuberculosis is diagnosed, and he gets more and more leave from work at the insurance company. Above all he tries, and often fails, to find time to write.

But all the chances of happiness he has, if they are chances, present themselves somewhere other than Prague: Vienna, and especially Berlin, capital of the early twentieth century. Here is what he said, in conversation, about the old ghetto, partly destroyed and partly rehabilitated in 1906:

> In us it still lives – the dark corners, the secret alleys, shuttered windows, squalid courtyards, rowdy pubs, and sinister inns. We walk through the broad streets of the newly built town. But our steps and our glances are uncertain. Inside we tremble just as before in the ancient streets of our misery. Our heart knows nothing of the slum clearance that has been achieved. The unhealthy old Jewish town within us is far more real than the new hygienic town around us. With our eyes open we walk through a dream: ourselves only a ghost of a vanished age.[8]

It may be that Kafka's smile, often attested to, is the answer to our question. The smile tells us that Kafka knew that ancient misery is not all there is. It also tells us he knew that ancient (and present) misery was not going to go away, and that new miseries were quite likely to come. Kafka told Max Brod that he sometimes saw our world as one of God's bad moods, or bad days. 'So there would be hope outside our world?' Brod said. 'Plenty of hope,' Kafka said, smiling, 'for God – no end of hope – only not for us'.[9] Many of Kafka's most memorable parables and fragments concern an immaculately pictured entrapment – the perfection of the entrapment being at worst a source of grim, self-defeating pleasure, a model of elegance in the midst of despair; and, at best, at its fabulous best, the mark of a heroic resistance, since the sheer intelligence of the picture seems more than a match for any trap.

> You are the homework. No pupil far and wide (*H.* 32; *G.* 82)
>
> The crows maintain that a single crow could destroy the heavens. There is no doubt of that, but it proves nothing against the heavens, for heaven simply means: the impossibility of crows (*H.* 32; *G.* 84).
>
> They were offered the choice of becoming kings or the couriers of kings. The way children would, they all wanted to be couriers. Therefore there are only couriers who hurry about the world, shouting to each other – since there are no kings – messages that have become meaningless. They would like to put an end to this miserable life of theirs but they dare not because of their oath of service (*H.* 33; *G.* 86).
>
> If it had been possible to build the Tower of Babel without climbing it, it would have been permitted (*H.* 31; *G.* 82).

In 1900, Prague had a population of about 450,000 people, 25,000 of whom were Jewish. Of those Jews less than half spoke German – about the same number (11,000) as the non-Jewish Germans (10,000). Assimilated Jews were lawyers and administrators, and in one sense part of an elite. But their social and civil position, never very secure, became more and more precarious. There were anti-semitic riots in Prague in 1899, and two of Kafka's sisters died in concentration camps during the Second World War.

Franz Kafka's mother, the former Julie Löwy, was born in Bad Podebrad, and came from a pious, scholarly Jewish family.

His father Hermann had moved to Prague from Wossek in South Bohemia, and set up a successful although sometimes uncertain fancy goods business in the city. The son of a butcher, he was a self-made man who never tired of saying how self-made he was. His name was a version of the Czech word for jackdaw (*Kavka*), and Hermann Kafka used the bird as an emblem on his business stationery. The name, according to Max Brod, was not uncommon 'among Jews whose family came from Czech districts, that is to say, Jews whose families lived in Czech districts at the time that the Emperor Joseph II ordered a census of all Jews'.[10] Hermann Kafka was not religious, although he subscribed to certain basic Jewish observances, like the bar-mitzvah of his son and (very) occasional attendance at the temple.

The whole question of Kafka's relation to his (and others') Jewishness is a vexed and complicated one, but it can be mapped neatly, as a matter of literary history, by mentioning that, at the moment of his first international, posthumous fame, in the 1920s and 1930s, Kafka was not seen as a Jewish writer at all and that by the 1980s it was very hard to see him as anything else. When Paul de Man, in 1940, wrote his troubling and later celebrated pieces in the Belgian newspaper *Le Soir*, he was able to discuss the inferiority of Jewish writing and the superiority of Kafka on the same page.[11] Kafka in those days – and not only Kafka, but any writer deemed to be any good – was perceived (at best) as writing in the pure, stateless style of modernity. De Man associates Kafka with Gide, Hemingway, and Lawrence. In the literary equivalent of the United Nations, the very idea of the nation dropped away, let alone the idea of a fraction of a minority. With the return of nationalism to the political world – but had it ever been away, except in our elevated fantasies? – nation and locality returned to literature as urgent topics. Editions of Kafka began to restore his idiosyncratic spelling and local idioms, the textual equivalent of respecting a Prague accent, and his Jewishness came under close, even obsessive scrutiny. The markers here would be Malcolm Pasley's critical edition of Kafka's works, the first volume of which appeared in 1982, and books like Ritchie Robertson's *Kafka: Judaism, Politics and Literature* (1985), Karl Erich Grözinger's *Kafka und die Kabbalah* (1992), and Sander Gilman's *Franz Kafka: The Jewish Patient* (1995).

Is this development an instance of historical progress or simply the swing of fashion? Well, first we should remember that fashion is itself often historical, 'a tiger's leap into the past', as Walter Benjamin says.[12] This means not only that the new may well be a revamped version of the old, but also that both new and old can be read as time-bound simplifications of more complicated realities. I would say that the recent passion for the particular has produced wonderful work, in Kafka studies and elsewhere; I would also say that the international Kafka was not just a fantasy, an idealizing error waiting to be undone. 'What do I have in common with Jews?', Kafka asked himself in his diary. 'I hardly have anything in common with myself' (*T.* 219; *D.* 252). This is a joke, of course, although a perfectly serious, even anguished one. We might think of it as a Jewish joke, wondering whether a member of any other community would express self-division and solitude in quite this way. 'The case of Kafka', Robert Alter writes, 'shows how a man may feel his way into a body of collective history through his very consciousness of being outside of it'.[13]

But then, although Jewishness would certainly not be denied in the joke, it would be affirmed only as radical separation – even from the Jews. This does not make Kafka an abstract or rootless writer. It reveals him to be a Jewish writer who is also international, international because he is Jewish – and because he is Czech and because he is German. The particular presses on us from all sides. Much of the conviction of Kafka's *Castle*, Alter says, comes from the writer's 'concrete imagination of uncertain steps and glances along the ancient streets of Jewish misery', but not only Jewish misery, and the work 'is surely not intended as a representation of Jewish experience'.[14]

There is a city in the south, we learn in one of Kafka's early stories, where people never sleep.

> 'And why not?'
> 'Because they never get tired.'
> 'And why not?'
> 'Because they're fools.'
> 'Don't fools get tired?'
> 'How could fools get tired?'
>
> (*SE* 9; *CS* 382).

'Our little town', in the later story 'The Refusal', is so far from the border that 'to imagine even part of the road makes one tired, and more than part one just cannot imagine'. But then this mournful little gag is topped by another. The border is unimaginably distant from our little town, but the capital city is 'even further' (*SE* 309–10; *CS* 263).

Kafka seems to have found the tone of many of his jokes in a combination of the Yiddish theatre and rabbinic tradition, but there are also echoes, everywhere in his work, of the great, grim paradoxes of Christianity. Christianity too, we need to remember, is a language and a culture as well as a religion. 'Most readers', Alter suggests, have sensed that the 'peculiar mode' of Kafka's fiction 'would never have occurred to a Christian imagination'.[15] But something very much like it occurred to the imagination of Kierkegaard, whom Kafka read avidly, and, as if in unconscious confirmation of this point, Alter himself, a page or two later, uses the phrase 'fear and trembling' in an otherwise explicitly Jewish context. I conclude from this and countless other examples that, while differences between religious doctrines (and between material cultural practices) can be defined with relative clarity, the imagination does not draw the same lines. The minds of many Jews are full of Christian imagery, and Christ himself, of course, was not a Christian.

Walter Benjamin said, in a letter to his friend Gershom Scholem, that the person who could find the 'comic sides' of Jewish theology would have the key to Kafka.[16] But Benjamin also connected Jewish folklore with German folklore, or rather saw Kafka as a meeting place for both. A great rabbi, Benjamin reports, said that, when the Messiah comes, he will not 'change the world by force but . . . only make a slight adjustment' . A well-known German folksong pictures 'a little hunchback' who haunts a child's days and nights. The hunchback is our displaced or distorted life, Benjamin says; his disappearance is the slight adjustment the Messiah needs to make. But the hunchback in the song also asks the child to pray for him, and this was Kafka's form of prayer, Benjamin suggests: prayer as a mode of attentiveness. In this consideration Kafka 'included all living creatures, as saints include them in their prayers'.[17] This is a secular, imaginary, ecumenical Messiah, one entirely suited to a writer like Benjamin, who began his Jewish studies with a book he had been given as a Christmas present. Kafka's own Messiah, indeed, was even more elusive than Benjamin's. He would come, Kafka said, only when he was no longer needed, not on the Last Day but on the day after that (*H.* 67).

Kafka's central comment on these matters occurs in a 1918 notebook, following a moment of what he calls *Morgenklarheit* ('early morning clarity'). 'As far as I know,' he writes,

> I have brought with me nothing of what is demanded by life, except ordinary human weakness. With this – in this respect it is a gigantic strength – I have strongly engaged the negative element of my time [*das Negative meiner Zeit*], which is very close to me, and which I have the right in some measure to represent, if never to counteract. I had no inherited portion of the tiny positive element or the extreme negative elements which may tip into the positive. I was not led into life, as Kierkegaard was, by the heavily sinking hand of Christianity, and I did not, as the Zionists do, catch the last corner of the fleeing Jewish prayer mantle. I am an end or a beginning. (*H.* 89).

An end and a beginning, perhaps. Kafka is more lucid than most, but this is the voice of a number of twentieth-century writers, and of scarcely any nineteenth-century writer I can think of. Even Flaubert, one of Kafka's great models, and who thought of little other than the negative element of his time, would not have claimed to represent that element in himself. He was its antidote and enemy, not its agent. He saw plenty of ordinary weakness but was not inclined to read it as representative strength. Hardy comes close to Kafka when he writes 'If way to the Better there be, it exacts a full look at the Worst'.[18] 'Exacts' in particular has something of the punishing perspective Kafka made his own, and it is more than possible that Hardy did not believe there was a way to the better, that his phrase is just a form of courtesy to old hopes. But Hardy wrote this in the very last years of the nineteenth century, and was in any case still possessed by at least the ghost of optimism. Kafka, like many writers who came after him (Céline, Celan, Beckett, Onetti, Brecht when he was not attending to his doctrine) knows only the negative, but believes passionately in that knowledge as a value. It will not save us, but it will save our understanding of disaster, and we shall certainly be lost if we deny it.

This is perhaps Kafka's chief discovery of that September night in 1912 when he wrote 'The Judgement', the result of the effort and joy and shame and the sense that 'everything can be said' – about love and guilt and ends and beginnings, and by extension about empire and weakness. The story opens on a note of modestly detailed realism and ends in a paralegal nightmare: a father sentences his son to death and the son executes the sentence. The scene is an unspecified city on a river, the time a Sunday in spring. From the two names that are given to us, that of the protagonist and his fiancée, Georg Bendemann and Frieda Brandenfeld, we may conclude we are in a German-speaking community. When the story begins Georg has 'just finished a letter' to a childhood friend now living and doing business in St Petersburg, and the first third of the story is entirely devoted to the context and content of this letter. There is much that Georg feels he cannot say to his friend, in his correspondence or in person – the friend last visited more than three years previously. Georg cannot suggest his friend return to his home town, because that would be intrusive, and perhaps not the best advice anyway. He cannot tell him how well he, Georg, has been doing in commerce in recent years, because, given his friend's 'stagnating' business, that would be tactless. 'So Georg confined himself to giving his friend unimportant items of gossip such as rise at random in the memory when one is idly thinking things over reflecting on a quiet Sunday' (*SE* 25; *CS* 79). The letter Georg has just finished would be an example, the narrative logic seems to say.

In fact, the story makes one of its several sudden swerves at just this point. What Kafka has discovered in this breakthrough work is the literary value of a form of logical restlessness, an appearance of nonsense or non sequitur that turns out to be the sudden altering of a premiss or a definition. It is as if secret panels were to keep opening to reveal the room we are living in as quite different from what we thought it was. 'Plenty of hope, but not for us' has the shape of this shifting logic, and so does this phrase from a notebook. 'Our salvation is death, but not this one' (*H.* 90). Unimportant events fill out Georg's letters, but not this one.

In this letter Georg tells his friend about his engagement to Frieda. Is this a good idea? Georg at first thought not. If the friend came to the wedding 'he would feel that his hand had been forced and he would be hurt', perhaps envious. Frieda says rather sharply that, if Georg has friends like that, he 'shouldn't ever have got engaged at all'. On reflection, and encouraged by an interlude of sexual excitement (Frieda is 'breathing quickly under his kisses'), Georg decides it cannot do any harm to tell his friend the whole story. 'With this letter in his hand Georg had been sitting for a long time at the writing table, his face turned to the window. He had barely acknowledged, with an absent smile, a greeting waved to him from the street by a passing acquaintance' (*SE* 26; *CS* 80). End of first part of story. End of anything resembling sanity in Georg's world. So far we may be a little surprised that Georg took so long to arrive at the place where we imagine most people would have started, and we are alert to the fact that the distant friend scarcely seems to be a person, seems to be more like an anxiously projected version of Georg's doubts about himself and his career and his engagement. But nothing we have read prepares us for what follows.

Georg goes into his father's darkened room to tell him about the letter he has just written. His father, who has been reading a newspaper, rises to meet him. 'His heavy dressing gown swung open as he walked, and the skirts of it fluttered around him. "My father is still a giant of a man", said Georg to himself' (*SE* 26; *CS* 81). The father at first seems mildly sceptical about what Georg is telling him, but then launches a full-scale attack, accusing Georg of lying to him, and indeed of not even having a friend in St Petersburg. Georg takes this as an attack of fatherly jealousy, or an implication of neglect on his part, and promises to look after his father better in the future. When he realizes his father seems seriously to be doubting the existence of the friend, Georg recites various details of the friend's last visit, including 'the most incredible stories' the friend told about the Russian Revolution. The father appears to accept this reminder as a kind of proof, and Georg carries him to bed and covers him up.

Things continue quietly enough for a moment. Apart from the uses of a restless logic, Kafka has also discovered how to make the most ordinary scenes and gestures escalate without warning into sheer terror. The father looks at Georg 'with a not unfriendly eye', and asks if he is well covered up, 'as if he were not able to see whether his feet were properly tucked in or not'. Georg reassures him, and the father asks again whether he is well covered up, and seems to be 'strangely intent upon the answer'. Georg says, 'Don't worry, you're well covered up.' Without warning the father shouts 'No!', flings back his blanket, and stands up on the bed, steadying himself with one hand against the ceiling. 'You wanted to cover me up,' he says. 'I know, my young sprig, but I'm far from being covered up yet. And even if this is the last strength I have, it is enough for you, too much for you. Of course I know your friend. He would have been a son after my own heart. That's why you've been playing him false all these years' (*SE* 29; *CS* 84–5). Georg gazes up, we are told, 'at the nightmare vision [*Schreckbild*] of his father', but his response is in its way as extraordinary as his father's behaviour. He has a sudden vision of his friend 'lost in the vastness of Russia'. 'His friend in St Petersburg, whom his father suddenly knew too well, touched his imagination as never before . . . At the door of an empty, plundered warehouse he saw him. Among the wreckage of his showcases, the slashed remnants of his wares, the falling gas-brackets, he was just standing up. Why did he have to go so far away?' (*SE* 30; *CS* 85)

More predictably now, or at least sounding more like many of the parents we know, the father sneeringly attacks Georg's engagement and his fiancée. 'All because she lifted her skirts,' the father says, Georg has besmirched his dead mother's memory, betrayed his friend, and tried to tuck his father away in bed. The father is described as 'radiant' with insight (*SE* 30; *CS* 85). For Georg's (and Frieda's) sake it would be good to see this radiance and this insight as an illusion, a sort of optical effect of the father's crazy, insulting exhilaration. But the prose is as firm as it is discreet. It does not endorse the father's insight, but it does not disavow it either, and that, as we soon see, is Georg's problem too: he has a version of his father in his own head.

The father now claims to have been representing the absent friend 'here on the spot', averting the intended betrayal; indeed he says he has been writing to the friend all along, and conjures up an extraordinary image of the friend receiving two sets of letters from father and son, crumpling the son's unread letters in his left hand, holding up the father's letters in his right hand, about to read them. Georg tries to defend himself by mockery, but without success: 'in his very mouth the words turned into deadly earnest' (*SE* 31; *CS* 87). The father describes Georg as 'a devilish human being', and says he sentences him to death by drowning. Georg rushes from the room, down the stairs and out of the house, across the road, and swings himself over the railings by the river. He hangs there, waits for a passing bus that will cover the sound of his fall, murmurs 'Dear parents, I did always love you', and lets himself drop. The last words of the story are these: 'At this moment an unending stream of traffic was just going over the bridge' (*SE* 32; *CS* 88).

All kinds of ancient legends haunt this terrible tale: Noah and his sons, Abraham and Isaac, Laius and Oedipus. But Kafka is dramatically rewriting all of them. This father is a Noah who is not drunk and not asleep. An Abraham who did not love his son more than anything else in the world would just be wicked, Kierkegaard says, a mere butcher, and in one of his retellings of the story Abraham pretends the killing is his desire, not God's.[19] He does this to preserve Isaac's faith in God, but there is no suggestion of anything other than tyranny in Georg's father, and certainly no suggestion of love. This Isaac takes the knife himself and does not wait for the appearance of the ram. And Kafka's version of Laius reacts merely with a kind of vindictive patience to the possibility that his son will kill him. He does not need a prophecy, he always knew the story. He does not expose the child on a hillside, he does not have to. All he has to do is keep asserting his strength and leave the rest to the child's fear and guilt. For Freud the lure and the danger of the Oedipus complex lie in the imagination of forbidden success: the boy kills his father and sleeps with his mother, if only in his dreams. Georg is a failed Oedipus; he does not get as far as the wish, let alone the wish fulfilment. Indeed, there are two scary figures of the father here, or at least two ways of interpreting the father's behaviour. In the first he would be a powerful but single, stealthy person, someone who knew his son's thoughts all along, always remembered who the friend was, had consistently been in touch with him. The other possibility – even more frightening, I think – is that the father is an unstable set of persons, a shifting constellation of different threats and dangers materializing, seemingly at random, as different characters with different programmes and accumulations of knowledge. Perhaps this is what a father is in Kafka's thought, what judgement is. Not just whatever you are afraid of, but whatever you cannot possibly expect, whatever extravagant and violent non sequitur will do you most harm, leave you most distraught, drive you to death.

Frieda is a sketchy figure in this story, really only a cue for what looks like sexual guilt, and the chance of an unthinkable freedom from family and memory, the pale ghost of a future that is not going to happen. But the friend is in many ways as important as the father. What can it mean that Georg should respond to his father's resurgence by a desolate vision of his friend lost in Russia? Why are father and son competing for the friend's attention, at least in the father's presentation of things? I am inclined to believe the father is right in one (only one) respect. Georg does not have a friend in Russia, not because the friend does not exist, and not just because Georg is projecting his own uncertainties onto the friend. The friend is also a form of doomed certainty, the frozen freedom of escape, what Georg believes his life would have been like if he had got away. It is difficult to tell the friend about the engagement because the friend's life serves the same purpose as an engagement: it is another life, and a life Georg cannot want. The father's competitive invasion of this life is a sign of the father's gigantic, irresistible reach – and of Georg's hopeless acquiescence in this reach. 'Why did we have to go so far away?', How could Georg himself go away at all if he already regrets any imagined distance from what he is trying to escape? 'How could it be far?', Kafka asks about the village in Tibet. If your mind has construed what is near (and familiar and habitual and ingrained and even horrible) as the only available reality, then everything is far, and also never far enough. There is no place like home, because there are no other places. And home, under such conditions, has all the strangeness anyone could need.

Georg has a strategy for dealing with the problems of his life, and one that looks very plausible. 'A long time since he had firmly made up his mind to watch closely every least movement so that he should not be surprised by any indirect attack, a pounce from behind or above' (*SE* 30; *CS* 85). Most of Kafka's heroes subscribe, in vain, to something like the same plan. In vain because, like Georg they keep forgetting their resolve, never think of it when they need it, and because – this is Kafka's joke on himself and his heroes – it would not have helped anyway. Just the reverse. You need all the surprise you can muster when your already gigantic father has expanded to fill the world, to cover all the contours of your guilt. Kafka's other heroes work even harder than Georg does at the taming of surprise, but they too discover how deeply and precisely they are in error.

3

The Taming of Surprise

> Today, at this very moment as I sit writing at a table, I myself am not convinced that these things happened.
>
> (Primo Levi, *If This is a Man*)

A man, young or of indeterminate age, in any case not old, finds himself suddenly in a situation of radical uncertainty. He is a passenger on a ship that has just docked in a foreign country; he is arrested early one morning; he arrives at night in a sleeping, snow-covered village. In the most conventionally literary of these scenarios, he has just had a conversation with a ghost; in the most fantastic, he has woken up to find himself transformed into a gigantic insect; in the most banal, he sees a man chasing another man up a street in the moonlight. These situations may all seem mildly or strongly Kafkaesque, particularly the one involving the insect – but when did we learn to see them that way? They appear in, following the order of my brief description of them, *Amerika*, *The Trial*, *The Castle*, an early story called 'Unhappiness', 'The Metamorphosis', and another early story called 'Passers-By'. But what truly belongs to Kafka, and marks him as the writer he is, is not the initial dislocation or nightmare but what happens next. Or rather, what does not happen next. The man, in each case, fails to hang on to the sense of strangeness the situation seems to call for. He treats it as if it were almost normal, or as if it could soon be made quite normal. As if he could be already at home where no one could be at home. He denies or hides his ignorance or shock, anxiously asserts his control of what seems manifestly uncontrollable, even if his control is only mental, a matter of seeing round the corners of all possible arguments.

And gets himself, in most instances, further and further into trouble as a result.

Was a simple refusal of the situation possible? Probably not, but there is some distance between an impossible refusal and a would-be canny embrace. What Kafka is offering us, I think, is the image not only of an ordinary world invaded by the extraordinary, but also of an extraordinary world that cannot be seen as such. An image, that is, of the desperate reconstruction of ordinariness, of ordinariness as a last resort. As if the notion of the ordinary cannot be abandoned, whatever happens to it. Hannah Arendt's phrase about the banality of evil comes to mind, at least as an analogue.[1] Kafka would be showing us the domestication of surprise or horror, an understandable, even touching method of trying to live with what we cannot manage, but which has the effect of making it all the more unmanageable. It is for this reason that Kafka's fiction often seems so prophetic: not because he foresaw the atrocities of the twentieth century, but because he already knew so many of our strategies for dealing with them.

Of course the details of strategy are different in each fictional instance, the scenarios play out with all kinds of swerve and variety of invention. In 'Passers-By', the dramatic set-up is quite simple, and the central figure seems actually to avoid involvement. An unusual success, by Kafka's standards. The narrator sees a man running up the street. He could intervene and stop him, but he does not want to, and will not, even if the man is 'feeble and ragged', even if a second man is chasing him and shouting. The whole story is narrated in plural terms, starting with 'one' and moving to 'us' and 'we', but this seems a form of rhetorical conscription of the reader, a way of removing potential dissent. What is interesting, and what converts the story into a miniature comedy of anxious ratiocination, is the flurry of reasons the narrator gives for our not intervening. He does not say, for instance, that we are afraid or indifferent, which would surely be enough in most circumstances. He says it is nighttime and we cannot help it if the street rises towards us in the moonlight. And anyway, perhaps the two men are playing a game, perhaps a third man is chasing those two, perhaps the first man is innocent, perhaps the second man is a killer, and we would become his accomplices, perhaps the two men have nothing to do with each other, perhaps they are sleepwalkers, perhaps the first man is armed. And finally, the argument concludes, are we not entitled to be tired, have we not drunk a lot of wine? The last words of the story are: 'We're thankful that the second man is now long out of sight' (*SE* 15–16; *CS* 388). This is a trick Kafka also uses in the story 'An Imperial Message': mental or logical time, the time of the multiplication of obstacles or arguments, also elapses in story time; the men have gone by while we were persuading ourselves not to do anything about them.

What seemed to be a story about an everyday street incident is a swift, composite picture of the lies we tell ourselves when we do not wish to be involved, a story about the ingenuity and fertility of our excuses. And about our relief when we do not need them any more, when the threat of involvement is over. We may, although we do not need to, connect these thoughts and this mood to Kafka's own hesitations about commitment, most notable in his desperate doubts about marriage. Certainly we do need to see that the story's precisely articulated structure of fear, invention, deferment, and relief applies, like a parable, to many situations in many lives, including Kafka's and ours. Staying out of trouble can take more energy than getting into trouble, and no arguments need more maintenance than those we wish to make seem casual, or self-evident.

In 'Unhappiness', the man who has been talking to a ghost has the following conversation with a fellow-tenant on the stairs of his building.

> 'What can I do? I've just had a ghost in my room.'
>
> 'You say that exactly as if you had just found a hair in your soup.'
>
> 'You're making a joke of it. But let me tell you, a ghost is a ghost.'
>
> 'How true. But what if one does not believe in ghosts at all?'
>
> 'Well, do you think I believe in ghosts? But how can my not believing help me?'
>
> 'Quite simply. You do not need to feel afraid if a ghost actually turns up.'
>
> 'Oh, that's only a secondary fear. The real fear is a fear of what caused the apparition . . .'

> 'But since you were not afraid of the ghost itself, you could easily have asked it how it came to be there.'
>
> 'Obviously you've never spoken to a ghost. One never gets straight information from them . . . These ghosts seems to be more dubious about their existence than we are.' (*SE* 21–2; *CS* 393–4)

Here there seems to be no possibility of avoiding or denying the initial situation, the involvement with the ghost, but the reasons seem to lie, as with 'Passers-By', in the combined constriction and ingenuity of the narrator's mind. It is not only that he cannot think of a way out of his experience or his fear; he has deft and amazing arguments that block off even plausible escape routes. He tests logic against experience, and then invents new confining logics. Thus the claim that we do not need to believe in ghosts (because they do not exist) turns into the seemingly empirical claim that a disbelief in ghosts does not stop them from getting into our room. The new premiss that ghosts we do not believe in cannot scare us is not challenged, only used as a new premiss about the real grounds of our fear. And the idea of settling this deeper, shifted question by asking the ghost itself runs up against a new thought about the nature of ghosts, a brilliant transposition of their well-known insubstantiality into evasiveness, even ontological insecurity. The overwhelming impression is one not of helplessness in the presence of the supernatural, but of the determined helplessness of an intelligence bent on self-imprisonment. It would be no good asking such a mind to think differently. It would only invent further, more dazzling non-solutions. If this protagonist is not exactly failing to hang onto his sense of the strangeness of the situation, is exacerbating it rather, nevertheless he is anxious not to be at a loss, trying too hard to seem *au courant* with the unbelievable. 'Obviously you've never spoken to a ghost.'

The opening sentence of 'The Metamorphosis' is one of the most famous in world literature. 'As Gregor Samsa awoke one morning from uneasy dreams, he found himself transformed in his bed into a gigantic insect' (*SE* 56; *CS* 89). Gregor is lying on his hard beetle's back; he can see his many tiny legs waving in the air. He wonders what has happened to him and assures himself that this is not a dream. He looks around his room and out of the window, is saddened by the rainy weather, wonders if he should go back to sleep, but cannot manage to roll over onto his side. Then he thinks about his job as a commercial traveller. 'Traveling about day in, day out' (*SE* 56; *CS* 89). He recalls his worry about train connections, the irregular, bad food, the casual human contact. Above all, about having to get up so early. He has already missed the 5 o'clock train. Perhaps he should call in sick? When Gregor's father and sister ask him why he is still in bed, he says he will be up soon. His voice is a little altered – it is later described by someone from Gregor's office as the voice of an animal – but at this stage Gregor has 'not the least possible doubt' (*SE* 59; *CS* 92) that the difference is just an early sign of a coming cold, one of the occupational diseases of the commercial traveller.

The story continues with its eerie, elaborate development, through Gregor's adjustment to his condition to a final family showdown and Gregor's dusty death. Here I want only to insist on the uncanny mixture of lurid change and selective continuity that Kafka is laying out for us. Gregor has an insect's body but a human consciousness – more precisely a human consciousness modified, over time, by its habitation of an insect's body. His tastes in food change, and he finds he enjoys crawling over the walls and ceiling of his room. On the other hand, although he cannot make himself understood, he continues to understand perfectly all the human conversations he hears and overhears. I am not suggesting that the horror consists in Gregor's preservation of human consciousness rather than his transformation into an insect, only that the precisely orchestrated patchiness of the transformation is what makes this story – which Kafka once called 'an exceptionally sickening story' – so memorable. Its most distressing and haunting moment perhaps occurs not when Gregor crawls away to die, which is bad enough, but when he momentarily rejoices in the removal of the furniture from his room, which will leave him much more crawling space on the walls and the floor. His mother is upset at the alteration, and thinks everything should be left as it is, so that Gregor 'when he comes back to us will find everything unchanged' (*SE* 80; *CS*116). Hearing her say this, Gregor is aghast at the speed – he has been living as an insect for two months – with which he has forgotten 'his human past', and he crawls up an empty wall to press himself against what remains of his old furnishings – namely, a picture of a fur-coated lady clipped from an illustrated magazine and framed behind glass. 'This picture at least, which was entirely hidden beneath him, was going to be removed by nobody' (*SE* 82; *CS* 118). Gregor has become a desperate insect – do insects get desperate, perhaps they do – and, worse still, an insect with a failing or forfeited human memory, a model of an almost too successful adaptation to the unthinkable.

The opening situation in Kafka's three novels is more difficult to explore briefly, since it unfolds in each case into a long and substantial (albeit incomplete) fiction. But we do find there, among many other features, the same premature or excessive adaptation, or attempt at adaptation – to the unknown, in these instances, rather than the unthinkable. Karl Rossmann, in *Amerika*, shows from the start a striking mixture of confidence and diffidence, resentment and passivity. He is a 17-year-old German who has been shipped to America because he has got a serving maid with child – although she 'seduced' him, we are told. 'German' here, as was general usage at that time, means stemming from anywhere in the German-speaking countries of Europe. Karl later says he is a German from Prague in Bohemia. Upon arrival in New York – in Kafka's New York, where the Statue of Liberty brandishes a sword rather than a torch, and where crossing a bridge will take you to Boston – Karl gets lost below decks, and meets a German stoker who feels he has been badly treated by a Romanian chief engineer. It is not long before Karl is an expert on the stoker's case and is arguing it with passion and eloquence before the ship's captain.

Karl has no doubts about the justice of the complaint, although he is crafty enough to conceal the newness of his acquaintance with the stoker. It is Karl's 'opinion', he says, that wrong has been done to the stoker, who is industrious, has served on many ships, and whose merits should no longer be deprived of their deserved recognition. Karl has no evidence for any of this except his own feelings for the stoker, and the little the stoker has told him. Many readers have found Karl's passion for justice admirable. 'I believe Kafka never loved a character as much as he loved Karl Rossmann,' Pietro Citati says;[2] Danièle Huillet, one of the directors of *Klassenverhältnisse,* the excellent film made from *Amerika,* sees Karl as a natural rebel, manifestly a good thing: 'He rebels . . . when he speaks for the stoker . . . he rebels as he breathes . . .'.[3] But Karl's passion looks far more like a compulsion to take sides, an unwillingness to wait for information. His swift sympathy for the stoker is appealing, of course, but it also seems fragile and a little frightened, based as it is on Karl's loneliness and a certain nervous German nationalism. Karl is particularly worried about the Irish in America – or he has been told to worry about them – and the stoker is indignant that a Romanian should be chief engineer on a German ship. Of course I am not suggesting there are not Irish thieves or nasty Romanians or badly treated Germans, only that ready-made assumptions about nationality belong to Karl's and the stoker's sense of their world, and therefore to what we know about them. Karl's passion for the stoker's cause – which is also a passion for the stoker as a new-found friend, since Karl's uncle, when he appears, says Karl has been 'bewitched' by the stoker, and Karl can scarcely bring himself to let go of the stoker's hand, and parts from him weeping copiously – seems to me essentially the performance of a disguised anxiety. Karl knows nothing about the world he is entering, but he is already talking like an old-timer, as if he could inherit worldly experience by pretending he has got it. As if he could step straight into the role of crusading hero, skipping all stages of apprenticeship. There is in him, as in the protagonists of all the other situations we are considering, a drastic inability to be surprised – or, more precisely, an inability to acknowledge or cope with, as surprises, any of the surprises that beset him.

This characteristic is even more visible, and more elaborately, ironically staged, in *The Trial.* The opening sentence of the novel combines various degrees of reliability. 'Someone must have been telling lies about Joseph K, for without having done anything wrong he was arrested one fine morning' (*P.* 7; *TR* 1). The arrest is a narrative fact, confirmed by everything else that happens in the novel. It is on a level with the information, given casually a little later on, that today is Joseph K's thirtieth birthday. But the assertion that Joseph K has not done anything wrong sounds like his own protestation of his innocence, even if it also comes to us as flat statement, and the idea of the slander is openly offered as a speculation, a plausible cause. As Stanley Corngold says, 'the narrative begins not with the first event of the plot but with a first interpretation of the event'.[4] All we know is that Joseph K has been arrested – and that, it turns out, is all he knows. The rest is the mind making claims to more knowledge than it has. Kafka does not say that K *has not* been slandered, or that he *has* done something wrong, only gets the prose to enact a little more certainty than anyone possesses in these matters.

We quickly learn a lot more about K's mind and moral habits than we do about those of any of the characters we have looked at so far. The prose is sympathetic to him and often, as we have just seen, silently adopts his point of view. But its angle is not always his own. We are told that it was K's tendency to 'take things easily, to believe in the worst only when the worst happened, taking no care for the morrow' (*P*. 10; *TR* 4). He may think this about himself, may even congratulate himself on his insouciance, but we are also told that it was not his custom to learn from experience, which sounds a little more like an external judgement on him. In any event, we may begin to wonder whether this arrest – a strange arrest, since it consists only of an official invasion of K's privacy, an announcement and an interrogation, and after that leaves him free to go to work and lead his ordinary life – has something to do with K's character rather than anything he has done. Perhaps this is what happens to people who cannot learn from experience.

'Arrested' here is, of course, being used in an eerie, almost nonsensical way. Kafka uses two words for the situation: *verhaftet* and *gefangen*. The first literally means held and the second literally means caught; neither really allows for the possibility of going on with your life as usual. K himself uses the term 'accused' (*angeklagt*), which plays an important part in the book later. But in this first chapter the other two terms dominate, and invite us to imagine a strictly unnameable condition: an arrest that does not detain, an imprisonment that is neither literal nor metaphorical and not even virtual but something like a change of moral lighting, a stark alteration of the unaltered life.

When K is summoned for a first interrogation, he is given a day and an address but no time. He decides more or less arbitrarily – because that is when courts begin their work on weekdays – to go at nine. We are then told again that he wants to get there at nine, 'although he had not even been required to appear at any specified time' (*P* 43; *TR* 34). He gets lost in an unfamiliar neighbourhood, is considerably delayed, and on arrival is told that he is late – not just late in general terms, but exactly an hour and five minutes late, late by the timetable only he is supposed to know.

This is not to say the court exists only in K's mind – the very idea rests on a distinction between mind and world that is not tenable in Kafka's world, and not all that tenable in ours. The eerie telepathy about the time of the session suggests not that K has imagined the court, in the sense of making it up, but that the court has thoroughly imagined K, in the sense of knowing how his mind works. The court is real, we might say, a formal institution as firm and brutal as anything else in this fictional territory. But it has many faces and forms and the ones we see are the ones intended for K – more precisely, the ones attuned to K, tailored for him, the way any indictment, however impersonally framed, is full of the personality of the accused. Unless, of course, the indictment names the wrong person, but K never manages fully to persuade himself that the court has mistaken his identity, only that the accusation is unfair and incomprehensible. 'I am not guilty,' K says towards the end of the novel as we have it. 'It is a mistake. And, if it comes to that, how can any person be guilty? We're all simply human here, one as much as another.' 'That is true,' K's interlocutor says, 'but that's how all guilty people talk' (*P*. 226; *TR* 210). It is how (some) innocent people talk too, once they have been accused, but that fact only deepens our problem.

In the opening scene K produces his bicycle licence and his birth certificate, but these do not seem to help. One of the guards who have come to arrest him explains how things work.

> The high authorities we serve, before they would order such an arrest as this, must be quite well informed about the reasons for the arrest and the person of the prisoner. There can be no mistake about that. Our officials, so far as I know them, and I know only

> the lowest grades among them, never go hunting for crime in the populace, but, as the law decrees, are drawn toward guilt, and must then send out us guards. That is the law. How could there be a mistake in that?

K says he does not know that law, but the guard simply replies, 'All the worse for you' (*P.* 12–13; *TR* 6). This looks like, and is, a travesty of the law as we imagine it in modern civil society; slightly less of a travesty of how the law often works even in such a society. It is a perfect picture of how the law works in totalitarian societies. J. P. Stern cites the phrase 'Why, do you think we would summons someone who has not done anything', and comments that this 'is not a quotation from *The Trial,* but the reply of a Gestapo official to a question by a Jewish woman who is about to be delivered to her death'.[5]

But a law attracted by a guilt it does not seek out is also a perfect picture of many other laws, mostly invisible and unwritten ones – the law of conscience as well as the law of superstition, for example, the law of the Christian (but not, I think, the Jewish) God as well as the law of self-tormenting mania. We are not asked here, as many readers of Kafka have felt they were, and as Orson Welles manifestly thought he was for his film version of *The Trial,* to exclude what we know of spiritual imperatives in order to sustain a critique of a giant bureaucracy. But nor are we asked, as many other readers of Kafka have felt, notably Max Brod, to forget what we know about bureaucracy in order to keep afloat in the spiritual dimension. We may all feel, at some stage, that we have to make such choices, but I am talking about a much earlier moment in the interpretative process. We need, at the outset, only to see that the same language can be used for a monstrous (and historically familiar) breach of civil law and for the ordinary relations of God and the troubled soul. We are more expert in both regions than we think; a lot less expert in working out what it means that they can share a language.

K is called for an interview with an inspector, which takes place in the room next to the bedroom. 'Joseph K?', the inspector asks. K nods. 'You are presumably very much surprised at the events of this morning?', the inspector continues, 'arranging with both hands the few things that lay on the night table, a candle and a matchbox, a book and a pincushion – as if they were objects which he required for his interrogation'. 'Certainly,' K says. 'Certainly, I am surprised, but I am by no means very much surprised.' 'Not very much surprised?', the inspector says, 'setting the candle in the middle of the table, and then grouping the other things around it'. The objects on the table are familiar, might lend themselves to an 'effect of the real' in Roland Barthes's sense;[6] but they are also given a disturbing aura, as if the inspector's apparent distraction were a secret form of magic, or a clue not to be missed. The objects also focus K's disarray, as if his mind and ours could concentrate only on things like these. 'I mean', K continues, 'that I am very much surprised, of course, but when one has lived for thirty years in this world and had to fight one's way through it, as I have had to do, one becomes hardened to surprises and does not take them too seriously. Particularly the one this morning.' 'Why particularly the one this morning?', the inspector asks. 'I will not say I regard the whole thing as a joke, for the preparations that have been made seem too elaborate for that. Everyone in the boarding house would have to be involved, as well as all you people, and that would be past a joke. So I do not say that it is a joke.' 'Quite right', the inspector says, and looks to see how many matches there are in the matchbox (*P.* 17–18; *TR* 10–11).

A little later the inspector tells K to think less of them, the officials, and of what is going to happen to him, and to think more of himself. And not to make such a fuss about his feeling of innocence, which disturbs the not unfavourable impression he makes otherwise. Generally, the inspector adds, K ought to be more reserved in his speech, a few words would do. K stares at the inspector, and is outraged at the thought of receiving lessons from a person 'perhaps younger' than himself, and at the thought of being rebuked for his openness. And he still has not learned anything about the reasons for his arrest or about the authority that ordered it.

I need to make very clear that I am not arguing that K is in the wrong, or that an injustice is not occurring, or that the inspector is not the representative of a corrupt and invasive authority. Only that K's inability to allow himself to be surprised is a liability, and that, as seems to be the case with the inspector, good advice may come from a suspect source. When K talks about fighting his way through life, mingling a sort of resentment with a sort of boast, when he is so emphatic about not taking the whole procedure as a joke that we know he must want to do just that, we do not so much judge K as get very nervous on his behalf. This is partly, I think, because we could well be speaking this way ourselves, and probably on occasions have done – occasions less drastic than K's, with any luck. But mainly – I am writing now of what seems to be the most immediate experience of many of Kafka's readers – we are nervous because at this moment we are not in K's position but eavesdropping on it, and we know that he should not speak this way, and especially not in circumstances like these. The special, intimate Kafka effect, which shows such an understanding of our ordinary and extraordinary fears and compulsions, is to hold K's troubling performance before us, and then give the logic a further twist. What K's behaviour suggests is not just that we talk too much when a few words would do. It is that we have only to realize that a few words will do in order to start talking too much.

Kafka's fullest development of the anguish and the embarrassment and – in its furthest, most ironic reaches – the comedy of this situation occurs at the beginning of *The Castle*. Here the stranger arriving in a village is completely ignorant of local conditions; but the villagers are also ignorant about the stranger – has he been summoned as a land surveyor or has he just wandered in? – and both sides conceal their ignorance in an elaborate and crafty show of authority and expertise. It is as if everyone were caught up in a spy novel of the kind that became so popular during the Cold War. The spy novel itself had, of course, been invented before *The Castle*, by John Buchan and others, and I do not know if Kafka had read any examples of it. He certainly seems to have intuitively understood and anticipated the whole genre all at once.

There are no rooms free at the village inn, but K, the stranger, is allowed to sleep on the floor of the public bar. Soon after he drops off, he is awakened and told he cannot stay in the village without permission from the castle. 'This village belongs to the Castle, whoever lives here or passes the night here does so, in a manner of speaking, in the Castle itself. Nobody may do that without the Count's permission.' K sits up, smooths down his hair, and asks, 'What village is this I have wandered into? Is there a castle here?' (*S*. 9–10; *C*. 4). The locals, a few of whom are still hanging around in the bar, shake their heads over this, or, rather more literally, over K ('über K'). If K is the land surveyor called in by the count, as he says he is a page or so later, why is he pretending not to know where he is? If he is not the land surveyor, but improvises this occupation once he sees he needs a reason for being in the village, what exactly was K doing a page or so earlier, in the opening paragraph of the novel.

> It was late in the evening when K arrived. The village was deep in snow. The Castle hill was hidden, veiled in mist and darkness, nor was there even a glimmer of light hinted to show that a castle was there. On the wooden bridge leading from the main road to the village, K stood for a long time gazing into the apparent emptiness above him. (*S*. 9; *C*. 3)

'Apparent emptiness' (*scheinbare Leere*) is one of Kafka's philosophical jokes, a sort of relocation of Cartesian doubt. It is not that we know what we think but cannot trust our senses, and therefore cannot be sure of the external world. The external world is definitely there, but our senses will not reveal it us, so we do not know what to think.

But more important for our present discussion is K's pause on the bridge. Is he looking up at the castle he cannot see, so to speak, or is he wondering whether the emptiness is empty? The possibilities are not equally balanced. The evidence suggesting that K knows where he is is stronger than the evidence suggesting he does not. The challenging question is why there should be any conflicting evidence at all. Kafka is not interested, we might say, in the theoretically undecidable – or at least by the time he comes to write *The Castle* he is not – only in the drama of mutually exclusive argument.

Here is how the show continues. Once woken up, K asks the young man who is challenging his presence in the village to confirm that permission is needed to stay overnight in the inn, and then, yawning and pretending to get up ('als wolle er aufstehn'), says he will have to go and get permission then. 'From whom?', the young man asks. 'From the count,' K says;

'that is the only thing to be done'. The young man is shocked, literally takes a pace back. 'Permission from the Count in the middle of the night?', he shouts. 'Is that impossible?', K asks calmly. 'Then why did you waken me?' The young man gets into a rage, but K now seems to have things under control. 'Enough of this play-acting,' K says, as if he was not doing a very successful stagy job himself. He says this in a voice that is 'strikingly quiet', a phrase Kafka also uses in 'The Metamorphosis'. K continues rather grandly, 'You are going a little too far, my good fellow . . .' (*S*. 10; *C*. 4–5). He explains that he is the land surveyor whom the count has called for, and that his assistants will arrive tomorrow with his equipment. The young man decides he had better telephone the castle for instructions, and K, now pretending to sleep, is surprised that there is a telephone in the inn. Then follows one of those sentences we have now perhaps learned to expect, where the logic itself mimes a kind of nervousness that will not admit how nervous it is. 'This particular instance surprised K, but on the whole he had of course expected it' (*S*. 11; *C*. 5). Of course. The young man is told on the telephone that no land surveyor is expected, but then almost immediately the telephone rings again bringing a correction. They are expecting a land surveyor.

We have had so far no real reason to doubt K's claim that he is a land surveyor, and that that is why he is here, but, in the eerie world of which Kafka has now become a complete master, we need only a confirmation that the world has accepted us at our own estimate to wonder whether that estimate can be right. The paragraph that follows the second telephone call is both poised and dizzying, a miniature model of how the mind makes and remakes reality in Kafka.

> K pricked up his ears. So the castle had named him as Land-Surveyor. That was unpropitious for him, on the one hand, for it meant that the Castle was well informed about him, had weighed up the power relations, and was taking up the challenge with a smile. On the other hand, however, it was quite propitious, for it proved, in his view, that they had underestimated his strength, and he would have more freedom of action than he had dared to hope. And if they expected to terrify him by their lofty superiority in recognizing him as Land-Surveyor, they were mistaken; it made his skin prickle a little, that was all. (*S*. 13; *C*. 7–8)

The brilliant, scary comedy of this passage is so fast and so intricate that I cannot do more than hint at its ingredients. The man who has just said he is a land surveyor now assumes that the acceptance of his claim is a matter not of truth but of tactics, a preparation for a coming fight. Why would there be a fight, why would it be anything other than favourable for your employers to confirm the fact that you are employed? Why would you have more freedom if they agreed you were what you said you were than if they did not? And, most striking of all, how does the idea of being terrified, and of wanting to terrify – *Schrecken* is a very strong word – creep into these matters of labour relations? We seem to be on the edge of allegory, but the allegory fades as soon as we try to give it an outline, and we are left feeling simply that the arena of ordinary events – arriving in a village, finding a place to sleep, taking up a new job – has been invaded by psychic weather blowing in from realms of extraordinary anguish. But there is also Kafka's smile lurking in the prose, a textual trace of the pleasure he takes in the rigorous elaboration of nonsense. It is as if Kierkegaard had taken over the job centre, and then a subdued and subtle version of the Marx Brothers had taken over Kierkegaard.

This alarming and amusing perspective becomes clearest at the end of the first chapter of the novel, when K's assistants appear. These are two manifestly local lads, known to people in the village. It is pretty certain too that K has never seen them before. So they become his old assistants because they say they are, and because he does not say they are not. It may be that they are his assistants in the same way and to the same degree that he is a land surveyor. Because, of course, if K had simply made up his profession and his appointment by the count, the crazy comedy I've described would not be so crazy. The people in the castle would not have recognized K's earlier, actual appointment; they would, at the precise moment of the telephone call, have decided to take up his bluff. All his canny and anxious thoughts would then seem fairly appropriate, except that we are still left wondering where the possibility of terror comes from. The conversation with the assistants is a masterly portrait of the negotiation of uncertainty, the cunning conversion of what might be, with a few hitches, into what is.

'Who are you?' he asked, looking from one to the other.
'Your assistants,' they answered.
'They're the assistants,' corroborated the landlord in a low voice.
'What?' said K. 'Are you my old assistants, whom I told to follow me and whom I am expecting?'
They said yes.
'That is good,' observed K after a short pause. 'It is good that you've come.'
'Well,' K said after another pause, 'you've come very late; you're very slack'.
'It was a long way,' said one of them.
'A long way,' repeated K, 'but I met you just now coming from the Castle'.
'Yes,' they said without further explanation.
'Where is the apparatus?' asked K.
'We haven't any,' said they.
'The apparatus which I left in your care,' said K.
'We do not have any,' they repeated.
'Oh, you are fine fellows!' said K. 'Do you know anything about land surveying?'
'No,' said they.
'But if you are my old assistants, you must know something about it,' said K.
They were silent.
'Well, come along,' said K, and pushed them ahead of him into the house. (*S* 27; *C.* 24)

This conversation strongly suggests that our second reading of K's situation is correct, that he is no more a land surveyor summoned by the count than these two are his old assistants. This possibility is not as reassuring as it might be, since it simply shifts the grounds of the mystery, settles one question only to open up a host of others. If K is not a land surveyor, why does he say he is? Could he be a real land surveyor, but not one who has been invited here? Could he be a real land surveyor, with a real appointment but only imaginary assistants – who have now materialized because he said he had them. In any case, why does the castle confirm him in his post? If it has not summoned him, why does it not simply let him go?

But, in the context of our investigation of the tangled relations of the ordinary and the extraordinary in Kafka, something is genuinely settled here. In *The Castle*, although K is precariously placed throughout, and addicted, as all the other characters we have looked at are, to the assertion of a control he cannot possibly possess, he is far less helpless than the others, less reckless than Karl in *Amerika* or Joseph K in *The Trial*, less timid than the characters in the early stories, less desperately adaptable than Gregor Samsa. K has understood, or has begun to understand, what the others were only groping towards: how one might learn to live with the extraordinary without normalizing it.

K seems to know, as the others do not, that self and world are neither perfectly matched nor perfectly opposed, and that we cannot contrast the fiction of the one to the fact of the other – either way. Characters in Kafka (and not only in Kafka) often behave as if the world is either just what it is or an elaborate conspiracy against them, an implementation of their bad dreams. What *The Castle* suggests is that both self and world are mixed packages, bundles of fiction and fact, truth and lies. They are, we might say, both conspiracies but conspiracies necessarily engaged with each other, and what we call reality is the result of their clash or tangle, nothing else. In such a context the ordinary is our name for the comfort of a familiar, habitual conspiracy, and the extraordinary is whatever rattles it. Of course, the effect of either conspiracy, and still more of both, can be starkly, even terminally material – even hypotheses get people killed.

Conspiracy is probably too violent a metaphor, but I am trying to dramatize the sense, very strong in Kafka but also in a number of other modern writers, of reality as an intricate set-up rather than a collection of objects or truths – solid enough, but held together by its articulations, not by the sheer gravity of its matter. 'The world is everything that is the case,' Wittgenstein writes.[7] I am not sure how much scepticism hides in this assertive sentence but it is clear that 'is the case' is not the same as 'exists' or 'is true'. Wittgenstein's later phrase for this state of affairs, also a perfectly idiomatic phrase in everyday German, is 'wie es sich verhält', literally what relations obtain, translated by G. E. M. Anscombe as 'the facts'.[8] The point in this context is that there are no facts in the German idiom, only connections or proportions. Kafka uses the same idiom in just the same way, and it is striking that when Gregor Samsa thinks of getting back to some kind of non-insect reality he thinks of 'die Wiederkehr der wirklichen und selbstverständlichen Verhältnisse,' (the return of real and self-evident relations) (*SE* 60), translated by Willa and Edwin Muir as 'real and normal conditions' (*CS* 93) and by Malcolm Pasley as 'normal, unquestionable reality' (*M.* 80). The world is everything that is self-evident, a set of self-evident relations. Or rather the real and the self-evident go together, confirm each other. A world would not be real if it was not self-evident.

Self-evident is not the most idiomatic translation here, but the underlying implication is interesting. *Selbstverständlich* literally means self-intelligible, and more generally means taken for granted, going without saying. In conversation you can use it to mean 'of course', or 'obviously'. What is to return for Gregor is a world to which you say: of course. Or do not even have to say it. The full context here is telling. Gregor is lying on his back, trying to be calm, breathing lightly. He is still near the beginning of his transformation, and he is thinking of getting up and taking the next train to work. Normality, he seems to think, will come back if he waits. He is wrong, but only because his insect life is a new reality, what is now the case, not because his old life was not real or the new one is a fantasy from which he cannot escape. This, I think, is what the word *selbstverständlich* helps us to see. The real, wherever and however it crops up, is only partly a matter of understanding. It is more a matter of habit, of not needing to understand.

K in *The Castle* becomes a seasoned inhabitant of a complicated reality – social, spiritual, psychological, political – constructed and ratified in just this way, while Gregor Samsa remains its extravagant victim. When a character in *The Castle* speaks of 'factual relations' (*die tatsächliche Verhältnisse*) (*S.* 244; *C.* 259), translated by Willa and Edwin Muir as 'actual circumstances', she means not relations based in material fact, but powerfully tilted social relations of a kind that determine many material facts and much else: things as they are in the world she knows, and not as they used to be or as one might wish them. The 'partial satisfaction' for K that Max Brod says Kafka had in mind for the conclusion of his novel – K dies of exhaustion, but on his deathbed receives from the castle, not a recognition of his right to live in the village, but the permission to do so, 'taking certain auxiliary circumstances into account'[9] – may be a bitter irony, but we could also read it as a narrative version of the very insight I am trying to articulate. We cannot receive official certification of our being at home in the world because homes and worlds are nothing more than 'the facts' of certain times and places – long times and good places, if we are lucky. But we can, K's example suggests, combine our own persistence and the world's resistance into a life that is our own, and no one else's. We do have to die, but not 'like a dog', as Joseph K cruelly does in *The Trial*. We cease to be victims not when we defeat or escape our enemies, but when we see how they got us to join them in constructing a world and calling it ordinary – or extraordinary, as Borges would say, reminding us how intimately so many opposites depend upon each other. The Nazis thought the extraordinariness of what they were doing would keep others from believing what had happened, and in part they were right. The survivors of the camps often had to convert the extraordinary into the ordinary in order to survive. We need to see that the ordinary and the extraordinary are not conditions to be pegged down and mastered; to get used to or be ambushed by. They are the terms through which we learn to acknowledge our surprises.

4

Memories of Justice

> What is the contemporary voice that enters into the language of the law to disrupt its univocal workings?
>
> (Judith Butler, *Antigone's Claim*)

'None of that', Franz Kafka admonished himself in an undated note, 'slanting through the words come remains of light' (*H.* 213). Every element counts in this haunting sentence. There are only remains of light, they are to be seen through words, they come slanting or slanted – *quer*, the German adverb, is related to the English *queer*. What are these remains of light? What does light look like when it comes slanting through words?

To read Kafka is to become involved in a shifting scene of interpretation, an array of arguments and decisions that often feel like jokes and are very funny; but are not jokes, not even riddles. They are glimpses of what cannot be seen, remains of light, reflections of an endlessly missing truth. Interpretation is both theme and practice, a desperate adventure for writer, characters, and reader. At a central point in his writing life, Kafka focuses much of this activity around a single term, a name for the words through which we perceive the slanting light. The word is *Schrift*, literally script, or a piece of writing, but also translated, according to context, as inscription and even scripture. Kafka associates script with the law, and leaves it to us to work out what kind of law, civil, criminal, secular, religious, is in question.

'The scriptures [*die Schrift*] are unalterable', a character says in *The Trial*, 'and the comments often enough merely express the commentators' despair about that' (*P.* 234; *TR* 217). 'Comments' (*Meinungen*) here are 'opinions' in the sense both of personal views and of legal or theological interpretations. The implication is that we can often get a meaning out of a text only by rewriting it; by revising it, perhaps invisibly and perhaps unconsciously, in the direction of our own thought. 'Unalterable' is not entirely literal here – any actor or textual editor or religious fundamentalist knows that scripts or scriptures are often altered – but not just a hyperbole either. The text or scripture is not vague, or undecidable in its meaning, it just resists our attempts to take it over. 'Unalterable' means it survives our alterations of it; gets altered but also stays the same, lingering like a reproach and a reminder. It keeps offering other meanings, the ones we did not choose when we made our interpretation, when we rewrote the text. 'The right comprehension of a thing', Kafka has the same character say, 'and the misunderstanding of the same thing do not entirely exclude each other'.

It is not that 'interpretation is nothing but the possibility of error', as Paul de Man elegantly said.[1] It is that the possibility of error, in many cases, is the meaning, and to fail to see how one might be wrong is to fail to see the unalterable richness of the text, the residue of implication that allows us to look back and see what we left behind. Sometimes we do not despair over the text's unalterability – do not despair enough.

In the year 1914 Kafka wrote most of what we have of *The Trial*, abandoned in January 1915; and he wrote 'In the Penal Colony', the most historically freighted, the most 'prophetic', of all his stories. In this extraordinary work a traveller visits a French colony in the tropics, and is shown 'a remarkable piece of apparatus' (*SE* 100; *CS* 140), an execution machine that not only puts prisoners to death but inscribes on their bodies the text of the law they have broken.

In the case that is about to be concluded, the words to be written are 'Honour thy Superiors!' The prisoner cannot speak French, nor can the soldier who is guarding him. The traveller asks the officer in charge of the proceedings if the prisoner knows his sentence. The officer says no, and adds, 'There would be no point in telling him. He'll learn it on his body' (*SE* 104; *CS* 145). A vast gulf of assumptions opens up – how could a body read a text through the locations of its wounds, in any language, let alone a language its owner does not know? – but no one pays any attention to it. The traveller says, 'But surely he knows that he has been sentenced?' 'Nor that either', the officer says, smiling (*SE* 104; *CS* 145). So he has no way of knowing whether his defence was effective? What defence? The office explains that in this colony an accusation of guilt is enough. 'My guiding principle is this: guilt is never to be doubted.' This man, for instance, was reported by a captain for sleeping on duty and for not taking kindly to being woken up by the lash of a whip across his face. 'If I had first called the man before me and interrogated him,' the officer says, 'he would have told lies, and had I exposed these lies, he would have backed them up with more lies, and so on and so forth'. 'Things would have got into a confused tangle' (*SE* 104–5; *CS* 145–6). The traveller reminds himself that he is in a 'penal colony where extraordinary measures were needed and that military discipline must be enforced to the last' (*SE* 105; *CS* 146). But we are already deep in Kafka's universe of altered logic and displaced emphasis. Why is this violation of judicial process more extraordinary than the presence of a machine that tortures condemned men by writing on their flesh? Why is the officer smiling?

A striking feature of the story is the tone of ordinary reasonableness in which what seem to be entirely unreasonable, indeed inhuman arrangements are discussed – we have only to phrase things this way to see the 'prophetic' in Kafka's work. The traveller, for instance, feels 'a dawning interest in the apparatus', as if it were a curiosity rather than a horror. The officer describes in cool detail the three parts of the machine with their 'popular' (*volkstümlich*) names. The condemned man lies on something called the bed, another part called the designer (literally the one who draws (*der Zeichner*)) receives instructions and formulates the text, and finally the harrow, an elaborate arrangement of moving needles, writes on the body for twelve hours. The officer mentions the bloody mess of the operation as the 'one drawback' of the machine, and complains about a noisy cogwheel, and the difficulty in getting spare parts. The harrow is repeatedly said to be at 'work' on the body (*SE* 108; *CS* 149–50) – the officer, in his way, clearly believes that 'Arbeit macht frei'.

Less luridly, but more eerily, the officer perfectly understands all the obvious arguments against his cruel system. 'You are conditioned by European ways of thought,' he says to the traveller; 'perhaps you object on principle to capital punishment in general and to such mechanical instruments of death in particular'. The traveller might feel like saying 'In our country we have a different criminal procedure', or 'In our country the prisoner is interrogated before he is sentenced', or 'We haven't used torture since the Middle Ages'. The officer then makes an astonishing move. He says these statements 'are as true as they seem natural to you', but they have nothing to do with what he is doing (*SE* 113; *CS* 155–6). How could they not? How could his sense of the standards of what we think of as the civilized world not affect his own assumptions? Because his whole mode of thought is dedicated to other principles; grisly, harsh, but perfectly coherent and passionately pursued. Certainly he is not just arguing for the need for special discipline in a penal colony. He believes, as the rest of the story makes clear, in the beauty and bodily immediacy of a form of punishment no longer imaginable in liberal (or even illiberal) modern societies. At one point the officer seems disposed to plead for his death machine as 'most humane and most in consonance with human dignity' (*SE* 113; *CS* 156), but this is only a possible argument he imputes to the traveller, and his main brief is quite different. He likes the mechanical intricacy of the machine itself, and the formality of the inscription, as well as the stern order the whole system represents. The old Commandant, the officer's mentor and hero, is dead; the new man is a modernizing sceptic, no supporter of the officer and his rigours.

The traveller thinks 'the injustice of the procedure and the inhumanity of the execution' are 'undeniable' (*SE* 109; *CS* 151), but he listens carefully to the officer's accounts of the ceremonies in their heyday, and the anxious reader is half-afraid the traveller will be won over, especially when the officer evokes the 'transfiguration' of the condemned man at 'the sixth hour':

> Enlightenment comes to the most dull-witted. It begins around the eyes. From there it spreads out. A sight that might tempt one to get under the Harrow oneself. Nothing more happens than that the

> man begins to decipher the inscription . . . How we all absorbed the look of transfiguration on the tortured face, how we bathed our cheeks in the glow of that justice, achieved at last and fading so quickly! (*SE* 108, 111–12; *S*. 150, 154)

The word rendered here as inscription is *Schrift*, the unalterable text. The body, the officer is claiming, has read the text in a way that the mind could not, justice itself has become flesh; albeit mortal, tortured flesh, in extremities of pain and on the edge of death. 'What is a mere guilty human life?' is the implied rhetorical question. A modest price for such an illumination, a lesson to us all, which even the victim enjoys before he dies.

The traveller, far too late for the comfort of most readers, finally makes himself clear. 'I do not approve of your procedure,' he says to the officer, although he admits to being touched by the officer's 'sincere conviction' even in the realm of error (*SE* 116; *CS* 159–60). And here comes the most insidiously disturbing moment in this infinitely troubling story. The officer, who knows that the new Commandant and his followers have no time for him, finds it hard to believe that this sympathetic-seeming traveller is not on his side – because, we presume, he finds it hard to believe that anyone who is willing to hear the whole story will not be convinced by it. 'It did not look as if the officer had been listening. "So you did not find the procedure convincing," he said to himself and smiled, as an old man smiles at childish nonsense and yet pursues his own meditations behind the smile' (*SE* 117; *CS* 160).

The smile again. It is that of a man alone in what used to be a fully inhabited, self-justifying world – an 'independent arrangement', as Kafka says of the world prior to metaphor (*T*. 343; *D*. 397–8). It is as if a slave-owner were to shake his head mildly over our failure to understand the elegance of the old system, the way it all came together, benefited everyone, including those it seemed to victimize. Times have changed. The machine needs new parts, the officer is scorned, the ceremonies are neglected, this traveller is unconvinced. The officer announces that the time has come. 'Time for what?', the traveller asks, but the officer answers only through his actions (*SE* 117; *CS* 160).

The rest of the story needs to be read in slow motion if we can bear it. The officer releases the condemned man and sets about putting himself in his place. He alters the instructions for the writing machinery – the sentence now to be written on the body is: 'Be Just!' – smiles again, undresses and folds his uniform with great care, although this care sits a little oddly with the fact that he then abruptly throws each piece of clothing into the pit reserved for the body. He breaks his sword, and stands naked, ready for the law whose time has come. The traveller's behaviour is also a little strange here. He bites his lip and says nothing, although he can obviously see what is going to happen. In a few lines of indirect speech, we are told that, if the whole procedure to which the officer was so attached was about to be abolished, then the officer was behaving entirely correctly. 'In his place, the traveller would not have acted otherwise' (*SE* 119; *CS* 163). The traveller seems to be applying some code of military honour, the one where the truant officer is given a revolver and expected to blow his brains out, perhaps; or the one where the masterless samurai falls on his sword. But Kafka's discreet dislocation of tone and substance means that this recognizable, even conventional notion seems mildly crazy. Would we feel it was quite right, entirely in order, if one of the last of the operators of the Holy Inquisition were to put himself on the rack?

The officer's devotion to the machine now turns into a weird intimacy with it. 'It had been clear enough previously that he understood the machine well, but now it was almost staggering to see how he managed it and how it obeyed him. His hand had only to approach the Harrow for it to rise and sink several times till it was adjusted to the right position to receive him; he touched only the edge of the Bed, and already it was vibrating . . .' (*SE* 119; *CS* 163). 'It obeyed him.' As if it were an animal or a subordinate. When the officer is settled on the bed, he cannot reach the crank to start the machine, but he does not need to, it starts on its own: 'the Bed vibrated, the needles danced on the skin, the Harrow rose and fell' (*SE* 120; *CS* 164). Even the noisy cogwheel seems to have adapted to the new circumstances, since the functioning of the machine is quite silent.

Silent, but unruly, insubordinate after all. Its cogwheels begin to separate themselves from the system, as if they are being squeezed out of the machine. A large wheel rises into view, falls from the designer and rolls across the sand. Then another, 'followed by many others, large and small and indistinguishably minute, the same thing happened to all of them, at every moment one imagined the Designer must now really be empty, but another complex of numerous wheels was already rising into sight, falling down, trundling along the sand, and lying flat' (*SE* 120–1; *CS* 165). Thoroughly absorbed by this spectacle of disintegration, the traveller has not been watching what the rest of the machine is doing. 'A new and still more unpleasant surprise' awaits him (*SE* 121; *CS* 165). The harrow is not writing on the officer's body, neither 'Be Just!' nor any other sentence; it is just stabbing. The traveller, and indeed Kafka's narrative itself, now seems to want to make a particularly grisly and scholastic distinction. This is not torture (*Folter*), 'such as the officer desired', but unmediated murder (*unmittelbarer Mord*) (*SE* 121; *CS* 165). As if the machine was not dedicated, in its very conception, to both torture and murder, torture as murder. As if torture was martyrdom, and murder merely immoral. The officer is dead, his body impaled on the harrow, on his face not the least sign of the transfiguration he so eagerly described as occurring in other cases. 'It was as it had been in life . . . What the others had found in the machine the officer had not found; his lips were firmly pressed together, his eyes were open, with the same expression as in life, his gaze was calm and convinced, through his forehead went the point of the great iron spike' (*SE* 121; *CS* 166).

In a brief epilogue the traveller visits the colony's teahouse, where the grave of the former Commandant is, curiously, to be found under one of the tables. Here we encounter another form of inscription (*eine Aufschrift*). The letters on the tombstone are very small, and the text promises the return of the old Commandant, whose supporters appear to form some sort of secret sect, since they currently 'must be nameless' (*SE* 122; *CS* 167). The traveller leaves the teahouse, and hurries to the harbour, where he takes a small boat that will transport him to his steamer. The story ends as the former condemned man and his guard try to board the boat as well, and the traveller repels them with a heavy piece of rope, as if to cut off all human traces of the event he has witnessed.

There is much representation of writing in this story, but very little writing takes place in the narrative. The sentence 'Honour thy Superiors' is not written on the condemned man's body, because he is released. The sentence 'Be Just!' is not written on the officer's body because of the machine's disintegration or rebellion. It is true that we have the officer's account of former glorious executions – the old Commandant gave priority to children at the spectacle and the officer himself would often watch the transfiguration of the sixth hour 'with a small child in either arm' (*SE* 111; *CS* 154) – and that he insists on the transparency of the glass harrow, which means everyone can see how the inscription is completed on the body, and on the combination of long and short needles in the harrow itself: 'The long needle does the writing, and the short needle sprays a jet of water to wash away the blood and keep the inscription clear' (*SE* 106; *CS* 147). The script is readable, then, and meant to be read; but not read or readable by anyone in the present time of the story. When it is read it produces the spectacle of an elaborate and ironic justice, a verbal matching of punishment to crime; but only a spectacle, and there are no spectators now except the isolated traveller.

And of course the spectators are not the central players here, or the chief readers, and we need to pause over the puzzle of torture as reading. It is improbable but not impossible that the officer is right about the transfiguration of the sixth hour, since pain has been known to be a way of illumination, and the lives of many saints suggest as much. But the officer is also asking the traveller to believe that each punished body knows its particular, graphically appropriate sentence, that pain, or rather the aftermath of pain, or a supplement to pain ('for the first six hours the condemned man lives almost as he did before, he suffers only pain' (*SE* 108; *CS* 149)) affords a precise, construable alphabet, a kind of Braille system of torment. What the spectators read through the glass harrow is grisly enough, particularly if we imagine the blood that is constantly washed away, but the act of reading even in this case is perfectly orthodox: one recognizes letters as they form, puts them together into words. But for the body to read an inscription through its wounds – to 'decipher' it, to use the officer's word – a special talent would be needed, a feeling literacy. The notion of writing as drawing is also important, and the simultaneity of the writing and the reading. The body reads pictures, so to speak, and reads them as they arrive.

There is a danger of being too refined here. Kafka no doubt wants us to remember the brutality of these procedures in spite of (or because of) the normalizing language the characters use. In one sense, the condemned man does not read; he is just cruelly tortured in the name of a fastidious, verbally infatuated legality. No one except the spectators and the operator reads anything, and only they are in a position to enjoy the irony, the 'poetic' justice. But it would be unlike Kafka to leave us with so broad a point, not to invite other angles of vision. The brutality and pain do not disappear in any of these other views, but the idea of the body reading remains, not as satire or inspired nonsense, but as a figure for a knowledge of the law that would be corporal and irrefutable. That this knowledge does not appear in the story except in the officer's affirmations, that it cannot appear even there except as a fantasy, a kind of transfer of the spectators' literacy onto the suffering body of the victim, that even if it could appear within the 'reality' of the story it would be inseparable from pain and death – all this may be understood as an expression of longing for the law rather than a refusal or undoing of it.

The attraction of the officer's explanations for the traveller – and perhaps for us too, in some none too flattering way – is their conversion of confusion into directness, elaborate argument into immediate action, and this point again centres on a script. When the officer says that his guiding principle is that 'guilt is never to be doubted', he recognizes that this principle could not be followed by a court that had more than one judge or juror, or was subject to a higher court of appeal. There is a grim unwitting comedy in the officer's account, and an impeccable argument against democracy, given certain premisses. If you need to make decisions, and care only about order and efficiency, almost any unchangeable rule will work ideally, as long as you are the one making the decisions. The present case is 'quite simple', the officer says, 'as they all are' (*SE* 105; *CS* 145). But the officer's, and the system's, gift for simplification is seen at its most stretched and most powerful in the exhibition of the drawings (*die Zeichnungen*) that represent the instructions for setting the sentences in the machine. They were made by the old Commandant.

The officer keeps the drawings, his 'dearest possession', in a leather case, and cannot let the traveller touch them. He holds up a sheet. All the traveller can see is 'a maze of criss-cross lines'. 'Read it,' the officer says. The traveller says he cannot. 'But it is quite clear,' the officer says. 'It is very artistic,' the traveller says, 'but I cannot decipher it' – that word again. The officer seems quite pleased with this failed result, and laughs as he puts the drawings away.

> It is no calligraphy for school children. It needs to be studied closely . . . Of course the script cannot be a simple one; it is not supposed to kill a man straight off . . . So there have to be lots and lots of flourishes round the actual script; the script itself runs around the body only in a narrow girdle; the rest of the body is reserved for the embellishments. (*SE* 107; *CS* 149).

This account of the text makes the idea of the body reading it even more fantastic – the very thought that wounds would allow us to distinguish between a script and its embellishments is dizzying – but it also transfers the scene of reading away from both the spectators and the actual condemned man. What the officer reads easily, what the traveller cannot decipher in the maze of lines, is a project of writing, a dream of the body become text. The drawings, ostensibly instructions for whoever sets the machine, are the map of an imaginary justice, where it is the script that kills, not the needles. What the law writes on the torn body of Damiens the regicide, described at the beginning of Michel Foucault's *Discipline and Punish,* is the power of the king and the force of an example, the public fact of crime.[2] What the law writes on the body of condemned men, in the officer's idealizing view, is a verbal truth that transcends words, an unimaginable proximity to the law itself. If his body had been able to read his own sentence, the officer would not only have been instructed to be just; he would have been converted into a living (and then dead) emblem not of justice but of its exclusive and mortal pursuit. The emblem would waver a little, of course, as emblems do in Kafka. Justice is not hampered, for instance, by any confusion between the script and its embellishments; the officer has no trouble reading the script. But the reason for the embellishments is merely contingent, a matter of filling up twelve hours (the script is 'not supposed to kill straight away'). The consistency of the human body appears to have distracted justice from its stark simplicity. And then, of course, there is no such emblem in the story as we have it: only the calm and convinced face with a spike through its forehead.

The old Commandant's drawings reappear when the officer sentences himself. He leafs through the sheets, finds the one he wants, and shows it to the traveller. 'I've already told you I cannot read those pages,' the traveller says. 'Just look at the sheet carefully,' the officer says, but that does not help, and in what follows the sentence and the torment are removed one stage further from the actual machine and the body, as if the very idea of such immediacy, in Kafka's world, could produce only more and more ingenious flights into the ideal. The officer now recreates his own reading by writing in the air, and by speaking it aloud.

> He outlined the script with his little finger, holding it high above the paper, as if the sheet was on no account to be sullied by touch, in order to help the traveller to follow the script in that way. The traveller did make an effort, meaning to please the officer in this respect at least, but he was quite unable to follow. Now the officer began to spell it, letter by letter, and then read out the words. ' "Be Just!", is what is written there,' he said, 'surely you can read it now'. The traveller bent so close to the paper that the officer feared he might touch it and drew it farther away; the traveller made no remark, but it was clear that he still could not read it. ' "Be just!", is what is written there,' the officer said again. 'Maybe,' the traveller said, 'I am prepared to believe you'. 'Well, then,' the officer said, at least partly satisfied . . . (*SE* 117–18; *CS* 161)

This haunting little scene pictures justice no longer even as a map, still less as an intelligible system or an inscription decipherable by the body. It is a text that may not be touched and that is legible only by those who know it already. We need to note the curious condition to which Kafka has brought us as readers. We share the traveller's frustration in being unable to read, even if we are not disposed to please the officer in any respect. But then, by one of those extraordinary flips of identification of which Kafka is the master, we share even more fully in the officer's disappointment, the sheer solitude of his knowledge of this (for him) admirable law and how it works. The pathos of this lone survival of a former legal system is in no way diminished – is heightened rather – by the intricate ferocity of the system. Even cruel and intolerable gods can be mourned when they are dead – especially when their death leaves the world without gods entirely. 'Slanting through the words come remains of light' – if we are lucky. Otherwise the words contain only our longing for the light.

We have seen how *The Trial* begins. It ends with the execution of Joseph K, who thinks of himself as dying 'like a dog'. 'Where was the judge whom he had never seen? Where was the high court he had never reached?' (*P.* 244; *TR* 228). In the penultimate chapter K encounters a priest in a cathedral, who informs him that he is deceiving himself about his case, and tells him a story taken from 'the writings [*Schriften*] which preface the law' (*P.* 229; *TR* 213). Kafka published this story, without context or commentary, under the title 'Before the Law', in his short story collection *A Country Doctor*, and it may be worth looking at this unalterable script itself before we see what Kafka's characters in *The Trial* make of it as interpreters.

The story tells of a doorkeeper and a door. A man from the country approaches the doorkeeper and asks to be admitted to the Law. The doorkeeper says he cannot let him in at the moment. Perhaps later. The door stands open, 'as always'. The doorkeeper invites the man to try his luck if he feels tempted, but warns him that he himself is only the least of the doorkeepers, and that 'from hall to hall there is one doorkeeper after another, each more powerful than the last. The third doorkeeper is already so terrible that even I cannot bear to look at him.' The man is surprised by this information, because he thinks the Law 'should be accessible at all times and to everyone', but he looks closer at the doorkeeper with his 'big, sharp nose' and 'long, thin, black Tartar beard', and decides to wait. Years go by, the man keeps asking to be admitted, the doorkeeper keeps telling him that he cannot let him in yet. The man gives the doorkeeper everything he has as bribes, but nothing helps. The man 'forgets the other doorkeepers, and this first one seems to him the sole obstacle preventing access to the Law'. He curses at first, later only grumbles. His eyes begin to fail him, yet even they can see 'a radiance' that streams from the door of the Law. He has a last question he needs to ask. 'Everyone strives to reach the Law,' the man says, 'so how does it happen that in all these many years no one but myself has ever asked for admittance?' The doorkeeper, realizing that the man is close to his end, says 'No one else could ever be admitted here, since this entrance was made only for you. I am now going to shut it' (*SE* 131–2; *CS* 3–4).

The most immediately striking (and daunting) features of this piece of writing are its low ration of anything we could call information, and its scrupulous closing-off of almost all reliable logical inference. What we can say for sure here seems to be only that the door is open and that it does indeed lead to the Law – we might doubt that too if we felt like it, but it is hard to see what would be left of the story if we did. The doorkeeper has features, including a Tartar beard, that seem unequivocally frightening, and we may wonder what experiences the man from the country has had with such types, and where. And – I do think some logical inferences are hard to resist – time and ageing play an important role in the story. The radiance streaming from the door of the law seems to arrive only as the man's eyesight fails, since there is no mention of it before, and the doorkeeper, for private or official reasons, appears to be able to answer the man's question only because he is dying. Perhaps the man can ask the question only now and for the same reason, but this is less clear. We are simply told that 'all his experiences in these long years' gather into one question he has not put yet.

Above all, of course, the sense of ironic exclusion, a kind of logical trick, is very strong in the story, however we read it. There is a door meant for this man, but he cannot use it. Plenty of hope, but not for us, as Kafka told Max Brod. The radiance shines but only as your eyesight goes. Or: there is a door meant for this man and he could use it, but a guardian is placed in front of it to tell him he cannot. The guardian will let him know the truth about it, but only when it is too late. The man should have known he was being tested rather than excluded. This would be a version of the Christian instruction that reminds us that the Kingdom of Heaven suffers violence.[3] Or: the law is open to everyone but abandoned, because no one cares about it any more or because all seekers of the law have been frightened off by its doorkeepers – if not the first one, then the second or the third. This door was not meant for the man from the country, or only in the special sense that it would turn out to have been meant for anyone who showed up.

In all these cases, and I think in any case we can imagine if we accept the reliable elements of the story as the ones I have just listed, the law exists but no one is known to have entered its courts, and this man dies at the door. I would want to distinguish this situation (all these situations) as clearly as I can from two others in particular: from one in which the law is definitely known to be accessible, if only to a few, indeed if only to a single person, and perhaps only in the past; and from one in which the law is definitely known to be quite inaccessible. In this phrasing I think we see the extraordinary delicacy of Kafka's doubt at its most precise. He also has related but different versions of the same situation, which help us to see both the range in question and the balance of 'Before the Law'.

In *The Castle* Kafka offers us quite casually the image of a person who believes he can see a long-lost jewel in a dungheap, 'while in reality he wouldn't be able find it there even if it were there' (*S.* 306; *C.* 328). Translated into the language of the Law, this would be to say that the man from the country was doubly deluded: he thought the law existed and he thought it was accessible. This is a bleak view, but possesses a kind of cool sanity, and it tortures us less than many of Kafka's other formulations. Not much hope, maybe no hope, and in any case not for us.

But in 'The Emperor's Message', a parable that comes from a cycle of stories about China, our chances are slim but unmistakably real. The Emperor, the fable goes, has sent you, his miserable subject, a message from his deathbed. The messenger sets out but is hampered by the crowds.

> He is still only making his way through chambers of the innermost palace; he will never get to the end of them; and if he succeeded in that nothing would be gained; he would still have to fight his way down the stairs; and if he succeeded in that nothing would be gained; the courts would still have to be crossed; and after the

> courts the second outer palace; and once more stairs and courts; and yet another palace; and so on for thousands of years.

Even if he made it out of the palace world, he would still only be in the crowded streets of the imperial capital. 'Nobody could fight his way through here, least of all with a message from a dead man.' And then Kafka writes his extraordinary last sentence: 'But you sit at your window when evening falls and dream it to yourself' (*SE* 138–9; *CS* 4–5) It is true that Kafka's word for dream, *erträumen*, has more than a hint of 'dreaming up', and that is how Malcolm Pasley translates the phrase (*M.* 175). We may merely imagine the message the Emperor has sent, indeed we may merely imagine the sending. But it is hard to resist the suggestion of an alternative form of knowledge in this story, however ironically and wistfully presented. We certainly cannot get the Emperor's message by any ordinary means, but that does not mean we cannot get it. Or does not absolutely mean we cannot get it. I do not think we need to believe that the odds are good. In the language of the Law, the man from the country is not going to make it through the door he has approached, and may not make it into the Law at all. But the Law may touch him after all and illuminate his life in other ways. Not much hope for anyone, but at least a scrap for us, as much as for anyone else. Slanting through the words come remains of light. It is true, and entirely characteristic of Kafka's tone and vision, that in many ways this faint hope makes for a more painful prospect than outright despair.

The haunting discretion of 'Before the Law' remains when it appears in its context in *The Trial*, but the stakes of interpretation are rather more immediately on display. The priest is ostensibly trying to show Joseph K how he is deceiving himself about the law and the courts. K is 'strongly attracted by the story', and concludes at once that the doorkeeper deceived the man (*P*. 231; *TR* 215). This matches his sense that the courts are playing with him, although that sense itself wavers, and K is far from convinced that he is blameless. As I suggested in the previous chapter, even the way he proclaims his innocence hints at a blurred rather than a clear conscience. What is attractive, presumably, is that K has been able to see a story about his self-deception as a story about his being deceived, but the priest tells him not to be in a hurry, not to take over the opinions ('die Meinungen') of others without testing them.

The priest produces a whole set of arguments purporting to show that the doorkeeper was only doing his duty, and indeed doing it well. If anything, the commentators or explainers ('die Erklärer') tend to think he was a little too lenient and genial in telling the man he could not let him in yet, since the phrase suggests the possibility of future admission. After two pages of dizzying quasi-rabbinical exegesis, which bring to mind Benjamin's idea that the person who could find the comic sides of Jewish theology would have the key to Kafka, K says, 'So you think the man was not deceived?''Don't misunderstand me,' the priest says. 'I'm only showing you the various opinions concerning that point. You must not pay too much attention to them' (*P.* 233–4; *TR* 217). The priest then makes the remark I have already quoted and commented on about the unalterable script and the despair it provokes.

The priest's advice is deeply contradictory or paradoxical at this point, since everything he says suggests that there are *only* opinions in such cases, and indeed this is his own conclusion at the end of the conversation. The priest goes on to lay out a lengthy opinion showing that the doorkeeper, not the man, is the one who is deceived, because the doorkeeper knows nothing of the law he is guarding, and, in spite of his self-important airs, is entirely subordinate to the man, since his only job in life is to wait for him and watch this door. In a particularly elaborate bit of scholastic finesse, commentators have discussed in detail the meaning of the doorkeeper's announcement that he is about to close the door, seen as problematic in the light of the text's earlier indication that the door is always open. Is he just claiming to do what he thinks is his duty, or is he tormenting the man at the last moment, seeking to throw him into 'grief and regret', as the priest says (*P.* 236; *TR* 219)? Most commentators agree that in any case the doorkeeper will not be able to close the door.

K likes this interpretation much better than the other one, and shrewdly says that, if the doorkeeper was deceived, then the man too, necessarily, was deceived, whether the doorkeeper planned to deceive him or not. The priest reports yet another view, a contrary opinion, (*eine Gegenmeinung*), which simply says the story gives no one the right to judge the doorkeeper. He is a servant of the law, and as such beyond 'human judgement'. The priest may mean – he is a priest, after all – that the law finally belongs only to God, or he may mean that humans are partial and the law is not. Either way, the argument the priest offers is now that to doubt the dignity and integrity of the doorkeeper is to doubt the law. This seems a desperately orthodox position and K is rightly sceptical. 'I do not agree with this opinion,' he says, 'for if one accepts it, one must accept as true everything the doorkeeper says. But you yourself have sufficiently proved how impossible it is to do that.' 'No,' the priest says, 'it is not necessary to accept everything as true, one must only accept it as necessary'. 'A melancholy opinion,' K says. 'It turns lying into a universal principle.' That sounds like a conclusion, and K pronounces the sentence as if it was. 'But it was not his final judgment. He was too tired to survey all the consequences arising from the story . . .' (*P.* 237; *TR* 220).

We know how he feels. The dizzying effect of the arguments is plainly central to Kafka's project. We need simultaneously to take the splitting of hairs quite seriously and to see the splendid intellectual comedy involved in splitting hairs in this way. This is a highbrow version of Alexander Portnoy's getting trapped in a Jewish joke.[4] But then something beautifully simple occurs.

The long conversation between K and the priest has suggested that interpretation is infinite (there is always another opinion), and that no interpretation can improve things for the man from the country; his deprivation of the law is terminal. But the discussion has focused on the doorkeeper and on what happens to the man, not on what the man does or could do, and the priest now asks K if he realizes who he, the priest, is. 'You are the prison chaplain,' K says. 'Do you want something from me?''I belong to the court,' the priest says. 'So why should I want anything from you. The court wants nothing from you. It receives you when you come and it dismisses you when you go' (*P.* 238; *TR* 222) We cannot assume the priest is simply telling the truth here, but the mere possibility of such a voluntary relation to the court undoes the grim opposition between truth and necessity.

Let us say the door to the law is always open. There is no doorkeeper, or rather different doorkeepers arise, in frightening succession, according to our conception of the law – because we cannot bear to think of the door as closed and yet no one seems to reach the law. These doorkeepers are not imaginary, and they are effective in excluding most of us, indeed maybe all of us. But they are not independent agents of a free-standing law. The court is neither just what we make of it nor just what it is. There is plenty of hope, and plenty of despair too, but neither will exist without our collaboration. In the previous chapter I described a form of joint construction of the world that involved accepting its notions of the ordinary and the extraordinary. The collaboration in question here is more positive, or could be, and involves our own idea of justice, and its preservation or loss in the face of repeated and undeniable defections from it. In the face of our own fear of it too.

We are ready for the world of *The Castle*, although Kafka and K are not quite there yet. K dies in the next chapter 'like a dog'. In *The Trial* either the court is more active than the priest says it is or K's capacity for self-punishment ultimately creates the only court he needs, since it suffices to produce two portly but indisputably lethal executioners. We might say, thinking back to 'In the Penal Colony', that the officer's lonely smile here takes on a frightening aspect of triumph. The traveller did not find the procedure convincing, but Kafka did, and put it into practice in yet another fiction.

5

Sleep and Society

> The only paradises cannot be those that are lost, but those that are unlocked as a result of coercion, reluctance, cajolery and humiliation, their thresholds crossed without calm prescience, or any preliminary perspicacity.
>
> (Gillian Rose, *Love's Work*)

Kafka is not usually thought of as a social theorist, and for good reason. The instigations his work offers to psychological and theological readings, to what Benjamin called the natural and the supernatural interpretations, are unmistakable and irresistible, even if they lead chiefly to bafflement – perhaps because they lead chiefly to bafflement. Of course, there is a huge social fact looming over almost everything in Kafka's fiction, and no one has missed it: the vast, tentacular bureaucracy, the labyrinthine system Kafka often called 'China', echo of the administration of Austria-Hungary and announcement of countless other faceless modern machines of government. But the bureaucracy is taken as given, a fact of life to be observed and hyperbolically (perhaps) portrayed – as if Kafka were simply following in the footsteps of his beloved Dickens, and had found, to no one's surprise, the Circumlocution Office in Prague. And indeed much of Kafka's work, perhaps most of it in this precise respect, matches this scheme. But in this chapter I want to pick up two suggestions I made earlier: that *The Castle* is radically different from the work that preceded it, and that it is different because it embodies and enacts a theory of society – that is, it not only shows us how people live in a social world, it shows us how a social world gets made and stays in business.

We have already glanced at the riddle of K's professional role in *The Castle*. Is he a land surveyor, and did he mean to come to this particular place, or did he just wander in? These questions are never finally settled; indeed the ambiguities are brilliantly sustained by a kind of meticulous vagueness on K's part, which the narrator of the novel does nothing to reduce. He has travelled a long way, K says more than once; he has memories of his home town with its church and cemetery, and the games he and other boys played on the cemetery wall. He talks about the sacrifice he has made in leaving home; he even mentions a wife and child. But how far is a long way? Where are we? France and Spain are mentioned in the text as places one could travel to, there are persons of Italian descent among the castle officials, and the architecture and climate of the village resemble those of Prague. Turks are named as legendary invaders, and there is a lot of snow. We are in Europe, then, let us say; or a parallel, virtual Europe. But that leaves us plenty of room. What town in the once-Christian world does not have a church and a cemetery? We know nothing of K's sacrifice except that he says it is one, and the phrase 'wife and child' (*Frau und Kind*) has a ready-made quality to it, like 'house and home'. We may think of similar pre-formed idioms Kafka uses elsewhere in the novel: 'snow and ice' (*S.* 116; *C.* 120), 'night and cold' (*S.* 118; *C.* 122). Willa and Edwin Muir translate 'Frau und Kind' as simply meaning home: 'When a man like me travels so far from home he wants to go back with something in his pockets' (*S.* 14; *C.* 8). K says this very early in his adventures, when he has just arrived in the village, and just learned that he has been taken on as a land surveyor, and it does have a particular note of bravado about it, since the one thing that does seem certain about K is that he has no intention of going home, wherever home is.

This certainty is confirmed by all of K's behaviour. It is his one consistency, and is focused in one of Kafka's most startling and unforgettable paradoxes, which K himself scarcely understands as he speaks it. 'And giving utterance to a contradiction which he made no effort to explain, he added as if to himself: "What could have enticed me to this desolate country except the longing to stay here?"' (*S.* 168; *C.* 180). The apparent contradiction is a compacted truth. Staying on, living in a country or a region, has nothing to do with the attractions that might bring a tourist there, and even desolation is not a discouragement. K was enticed not by a place but by a desire: the desire for a place where he could stay. It is true that K, quite late in the novel, mentions his preconceptions about the castle authorities, the ideas he had about them before he came, and it is also true that his staring up into the 'apparent emptiness' in the opening paragraph makes sense only if he thinks there might be something there. K's idea of somewhere to stay, then, includes a castle and its accompanying, hierarchical authorities, but if we think of the castle as an administrative unit rather than a building, as a place of permissions granted or refused rather than a piece of Middle European architecture, his idea would scarcely distinguish K from any asylum-seeker, or any other person who cannot go home or has not got a home.

Of course K is not quite an asylum-seeker. He does not appear to be on the run, or in any exile except the one he has imposed on himself. He probably is not a land surveyor, except in the sense I suggested in an earlier chapter: he calls himself one, and the castle takes him at his word. But even this is not sure. Avital Ronell sees K as 'Kafka's final and most valiant hero', a figure in the prehistory of deconstruction, who is just astonished at the 'radically arbitrary assignment' of titles and meaning in this place.[1] It is not that he is not a land surveyor; it is that the very term has no fixed sense. What is sure is the following zany set of propositions: K has been accepted by the castle as a land surveyor: the castle has no need at all of a land surveyor; K is never going to be given any work as a land surveyor; this does not really bother K, since what matters to him is not the job but access to the castle. When an official, late in the novel, formulates what would logically seem to be the central problem – 'You are a land surveyor and have no land-surveying to do' (*S.* 313; *C.* 336) – not only does K think the man's interest is 'dilettantish', but we ourselves have so thoroughly learned our social lessons with K, so thoroughly absorbed the habits of thought of the natives of this world, that we too are sure this is not the issue, was never the issue. How this has happened is a crucial aspect of what I am calling Kafka's social theory.

What can access to the castle mean for K, if it does not mean the employment he says he sought? The natural and supernatural interpretations beckon particularly strongly here in the form of neat allegories. The castle is the father's forgiveness; the castle is God's grace. I am going to try and avoid allegory, and abandon the literal only for the realm of incidental metaphor or analogy, and I shall say the castle is not something K could reach or fail to reach but a partner in a relationship that initially excludes K and ultimately absorbs him without giving him full citizenship. The castle and the village form a social world, to which K is a stranger. 'You are not from the castle,' he is told by Gardena, the landlady of the inn he first arrives at, 'you are not from the village, you aren't anything'. Then she corrects herself: 'Or rather, unfortunately, you are something, a foreigner' (*S.* 63; *C.* 63). Some time earlier, the village schoolteacher, responding to K's own sense of his isolation ('I do not belong with the peasants or, I suppose, with the castle'), remarks rather sharply that there is 'no difference' (*S.* 19; *C.* 14) between the peasants and the castle, and of course this is true as far as K is concerned: he is equally removed from both. But the social world K seeks to enter is based very precisely on the difference between the peasants (or the village) and the castle, and consists entirely of patterns of behaviour generated by this difference. Very roughly: the castle governs the village but chiefly by means of the village's imagination of what the castle wants. This sounds a little fantastic, but we may pause to wonder, without straying too far into contemporary political theory, whether any but the most violent police state is governed in any other way. In a more extreme version of the same idea, Kafka suggests that no one is more loyal to the old emperor of China than those among his scattered, distant subjects who do not even know he is dead.

But Kafka does not assert this idea in *The Castle*. He allows K to wander into a world that is structured by it, to learn very gradually the language and manners of this world, until he knows them like the native he will never be. And then Kafka shows us, with great patience and wit and a colossal comic sadness, how the social conspiracy, the conspiracy that is society, is formed. 'There is no outside,' as Wittgenstein said in another context. And not much hope of changing the inside, Kafka suggests. Plenty of hope for God, but He is not in here.

* * *

Kafka's showing of the conspiracy centres on Amalia, one of the sisters of Barnabas, whom the castle has assigned to K as a messenger. The whole family, father, mother, son, two daughters, is a kind of social ruin when K first encounters it. The parents are ancient and decrepit, unable to dress or feed themselves, the son does not really know what to do with his job as messenger, or even if the messages he carries are real messages, Olga, the older sister, hangs out with the roughest of the servants of the castle officials, and Amalia keeps herself entirely aloof, apparently locked in a sense of her own superiority. Whenever K mentions the members of this family to any of the other villagers, they are all horrified at the mere thought of contact with these people, as if they were untouchables, or bearers of some sort of social disease. Gardena cries out 'That scum' when K brings up the name, 'That rascally scum' (*S.* 68; *C.* 68). Her word in German is *Lumpen*, as in *Lumpenproletariat*. K's fiancée Frieda, a woman he has met and set up house with, describes Amalia as 'shameless' (*S.* 298; *C.* 319), and thinks his even visiting that family brings 'shame' (*S.* 299; *C.* 320) on her. What has happened?

It is very much part of Kafka's design that we get to know the moral climate of the village before we are told Amalia's story, which emerges only in the last third of the novel. There is a kind of three-way conversation going on here, or a three-part fugue, where the tunes offer curious inversions and echoes of each other. There are the assumptions of most of the people of the village, which we may think of as the local norm; there is the behaviour of Amalia, which we have to think of as aberrant by local standards but which seems to meet normal expectations for many other places; and there are whatever beliefs and criteria we bring to the imagined world of the novel, the deep but relatively unconsidered grounds on which we are, say, shocked or troubled or unsurprised by what is going on. All of these assumptions, norms, expectations, beliefs, and criteria, in this case, have to do with sex, and the notionally appropriate, if unequal, relations between men and women.

K has received a letter of appointment from a castle official called Klamm, a masterpiece of obfuscation and condescension disguised as civility. It begins, 'My dear sir, As you know, you have been engaged for the Count's service . . .' (*S*. 33; *C*. 30). The signature is illegible. K, reasonably enough, thinks he should talk to Klamm at some stage, but he never does, and his unavailing attempts to get into the castle might also be thought of as a long, failed quest for Klamm. Klamm grows in stature, in other words, because he is endlessly talked about and scarcely ever seen, and then only for a second, through a peephole in a door. Klamm is asleep at the time.

But Frieda, whom K meets at a village inn much frequented by castle folk, is Klamm's mistress, and the fugue starts here. No one thinks of her relation with Klamm as anything other than the highest honour, and indeed Frieda's attraction for K is inseparable from her association with the elusive official. Later in the book, Frieda's charms fade, she seems to 'wilt' in K's arms through her absence from Klamm (*S*. 167; *C*. 179); and later still, in a delicate irony, she is said to be 'respectable in any case' (*respektabel auf jeden Fall*) (*S*. 288; *C*. 307), because she was once Klamm's mistress. We do not know why she is abruptly willing to forgo such an honour and roll on the floor beneath the bar with K in a small-scale orgy of sexual self-forgetting, but she does, and of course she cannot return to Klamm after that. She and K move into the inn K first arrived at, and here, in a long conversation with the landlady, K is treated to an exposition of the full-blown Klamm mystique.

Gardena was also Klamm's mistress – twenty years ago, it is true, and he sent for her only three times. But those were the proudest days of her life, and she still keeps her tiny mementoes, including a photograph of the messenger who summoned her. Then she married, and for many years she and her husband talked of nothing else but Klamm and why he never sent for her again – presumably because even the fallen glory of her position was a kind of dowry. Gardena is not entirely sure that Frieda was Klamm's mistress. He used to call out her name, and that in itself was the honour of a lifetime, now squandered on K, but did Klamm do more than that, and does that constitute a relation? Gardena is one of Kafka's great comic hair-splitters, a sort of G. E. Moore or J. L. Austin tangled in an excessive appetite for Midrash. She wonders, for instance, whether Klamm ever actually speaks to anyone in the village, and whether his calling out a name constitutes speaking, or even calling in the ordinary sense. 'Who knows his intentions?', she asks, 'Wer kennt seine Absichten?' 'The fact that he used to call Frieda does not necessarily mean what one might think, he simply uttered the name "Frieda", that she naturally came to him at once was her affair, and that she was admitted to his presence without let or hindrance was Klamm's kindness, but that he actually called her is more than one can maintain' (*S.* 64; *C.* 64). K is startled by all this, and speaks of a 'terrible fidelity' to Klamm (*S.* 100; *C.* 104), but he means only the awesome sexual outranking of all other men by a castle official; he has no objection to predatory male sexuality in itself; how could he, since he also is its beneficiary? When Olga, Amalia's sister, later says that castle officials are always loved, that for them there is no such thing as unhappy, that is unrequited love (*S.* 240; *C.* 256), she is expressing a kind of rule of the community, an irresistible *droit de seigneur*. A woman would have to be mad to refuse a proposition from an official, or at least blind to the very currency of prestige in her world.

I do not know how much we acquiesce in this as we read, and what kind of judgements we are ready to make. My own experience, at least on early readings of *The Castle*, was that I could not yet judge this community because I was too involved in trying to figure it out: like the anthropologist anxious not to impose his or her views on an alien world, or, more precisely, like the player in a dangerous game who needs self-defence more than he or she needs morals. And, of course, there are worldly analogues for what is happening in *The Castle*, as my use of the phrase *droit de seigneur* suggests, many of them less violent than that. There are the older European courts, where the king's mistresses exerted enormous power; there are the newer Hollywood studios, where attractive women once used to sleep their way to eminence. And there must be countless unsung Klamms and Friedas in the businesses and bureaucracies of the entire contemporary world, along with all the ones who regularly make it into the newspapers. Even so, the picture Kafka offers is startling, and all the more so because it is offered as entirely self-evident, the way things are in the village and the castle, a set of manners and habits K must learn. Sexual favours are demanded (by men) and granted (by women), and the very demand is made to look like an act of grace, a form of election. Frieda's respectability and Gardena's regrets are small expressions of an extensive social ethos, and the fact that these extraordinary sexual powers are possessed by petty officials is one of Kafka's sly jokes, not only about different cultures but about relative morality within a single culture. Even in our world, otherwise upstanding citizens might find a rock star or a film star irresistible if the call came, but it would be merely ludicrous to go weak at the knees at the thought of, say, an insurance broker just because he worked in insurance.

There is no suggestion that castle officials are powerful and attractive in themselves; their power and attraction lie in the fact that they are castle officials. We may think of the aphorism I quoted earlier, about the crows who maintained that a single crow could destroy the heavens, and were right, except in one particular, decisive in terms of their world, where heaven means 'impossibility of crows'. Similarly, one refusal of the amorous advances of a castle official would reveal the whole system of demand and submission to be the implementation of a collective fantasy, a self-perpetuating dream, like racial superiority or the innate manliness of men. But this cannot happen because the castle means, among other things: no refusals.

But Amalia does refuse, and her story is told to K in detail by her sister Olga. Her refusal is not the exception that proves the rule; it is the unnameable case that allows the rule to continue as if no one had questioned it. Amalia and her family attend a local festivity in which castle and village come together to celebrate. The occasion is the dedication of a new fire engine for the castle, and Amalia's father, only three years ago a 'relatively young man', we are told, is a senior figure in the parallel fire brigade in the village. Amalia catches the eye of a diminutive official called Sortini – not to be confused, locals insist, with another official called Sordini. The names are a piece of entirely characteristic comic mischief on Kafka's part, since outside his onslaught on Amalia nothing whatsoever is known about Sortini except that his name resembles Sordini's: this is a red herring disguised as a red herring. The next day Sortini sends a messenger to Amalia's house with a peremptory, vulgar letter commanding her to come to him. The last words of the letter are 'Or else'. Amalia finds this summons offensive, as no doubt many women in many places would. Anyone who read this letter, Olga says, would regard the recipient as dishonoured (*S.* 235; *C.* 250). K himself, forgetting all he has learned about the local mores, indeed forgetting his own attachment to an official's mistress, is indignant when he hears the tale, and says he trusts Amalia's father lodged a strong complaint with the authorities. A little later, regaining perspective, K wants to distinguish between an offensive letter written to an unwilling woman and the affair between Klamm and Frieda, which he now romanticizes. Frieda loved Klamm, he says, as if that made all the difference. It is at this point that Olga says officials are always loved, and eclipses K's distinction by simply asking if he imagines that Klamm could not have written such a letter to Frieda, and if she would not have gone to him if he had.

Amalia tears the letter up, and throws the pieces in the envoy's face, and this 'insult to the messenger' (*S.* 249; *C.* 264), as the event comes to be called, is the start of the family's terrible troubles. More precisely, as Olga says, sharing in the mania for interpretative refinement that Kafka lavishes on so many of his characters, 'the curse on the family' (*S.* 236; *C.* 252) begins when Amalia refuses to go to Sortini, since the tearing-up of the letter could have been hushed up if necessary. Now no one wishes to be associated with the family, debts are called in, friendships are cancelled, the family's once-flourishing shoe-mending business fails for lack of customers, the father is ousted from the fire brigade – the unit has to worry about its 'purity', we learn in a resonant phrase (*S.* 249; *C* 264). K wonders where the influence of the castle is in all this. What Olga has told him about so far, he says, 'is simply thoughtless fear, malicious pleasure in a neighbour's distress, unreliable friendships, things that can be found anywhere' (*S.* 249; *C.* 265). Olga says no one is to blame, everything was the castle's influence, 'everything comes from the castle', (*alles geht vom Schloß aus*) (*S.* 245; *C.* 260). These two views are not as far apart as they seem, they are more like alternative descriptions of a single phenomenon than rival explanations of it. The castle does not act because it does not need to act. The villagers have only to feel the possibility of an offence against the castle in order to take action on what they assume to be the castle's behalf. The castle, in this sense, is like a version of the court in *The Trial*, except that its proceedings are not secret or permissive, they are non-existent. But without the idea of the castle, and its power of approval or disapproval, the villagers would not have acted as they did. Or, to put that the other way round, the castle is the name of the invisible law that the villagers obey. The castle, in its daily functioning a humdrum and self-important bureaucracy, also represents the indispensable idea the villagers have of themselves. Amalia's definition of what individual villagers like Frieda are doing when they despise her family is not enmity or prejudice but 'simply a recitation of common opinion' (*S*. 207; *C*. 221). 'Recitation' is literally 'praying after', (*Nachbeten*), as in 'Say this prayer after me'.

The members of her family never deny Amalia, or say she was wrong. But if the choice had been theirs, they would have decided differently. Olga says that she would certainly have gone to Sortini if he had sent for her, and that her father would no doubt gladly have sacrificed 'everything he had' (*S*. 252; *C*. 268), including his daughter presumably, to an admired official. Later the father vainly seeks 'forgiveness' from the castle, and talks of winning back Amalia's 'honour' (*S*. 259; *C*. 275), but these moves take us deep into Kafka's full-scale inversion of values, and obviously represent a desperate endorsement of the shabby local morality. Olga, who says she now understands Amalia better than she did at the time of these events, calls her father's efforts a 'betrayal' (*S*. 258; *C*. 274) of Amalia, and the term is not too strong. We need to linger on an earlier moment, before the hideous consensus closes.

When Olga speaks of the 'fate' (*Schicksal*) of the family – elsewhere she uses the word 'doom' (*Verhängnis*) – she is not saying Amalia should have responded when Sortini called; far from it. 'If she had gone', Olga insists, 'I should of course have thought she was right; but her not going was heroic' (*S*. 237; *C*. 252). But Olga does see that Amalia's not going was objectively the basis of the family ruin, and that one cannot argue with what has happened – the already occurred is the form of fate to which even Greek gods were subject. Olga's thought at this stage has all the despairing sanity so often found in the relatives of those who make heroic gestures, and Kafka is very close to the perception Brecht articulates in his *Galileo*: countries are lucky if they have heroes, but they are even luckier if they do not need them.

The central feature of the story is not Amalia's refusal of Sortini's summons, and not the village's abandonment of the family, which turns its members into paupers and pariahs, although of course these events are crucial. The discreet, almost slyly placed central feature is the family's failure to find the strength to combat the village's verdict. This is Kafka's most subtle piece of social theorizing, and the passage is worth quoting at some length.

> That was the time [Olga says] when people first began to despise us in the way you can see now. They saw that we hadn't the strength to work our way out of the scandal, and they were irritated. They didn't underestimate the difficulty of our fate, though they didn't know exactly what it was, and they knew that probably they wouldn't have withstood the test any better themselves, but that made it only all the more needful to keep completely clear of us – if we had triumphed they would have honored us correspondingly, but since we failed they turned what had only been a temporary measure into a final resolve, and cut us off from the community for ever. We were no longer spoken of as ordinary human beings. (*S*. 257; *C*. 273)

It is not at all clear what the family could have done, what the 'strength' they did not have would have consisted of, but it is clear that, if Olga is right in her diagnosis, we cannot simply condemn the creepy orthodoxy of the villagers and celebrate Amalia's lonely virtue. We cannot be surprised at the family's behaviour either. They are social creatures, this village is their world, and they were quite unprepared for their role as unintentional rebels. They reached the limits of their energy and resistance; how could they know that those limits would be so decisive? They could have got over the scandal, Olga says, taken up their old connections, restarted their business; their friends would have come back to them, their old position in the village would have been re-established. This may be a fantasy, but in any case the family did not attempt this mode of return – could not attempt it, because they were so scandalized themselves, and because, for all their loyalty to Amalia, they did not understand her action at all. They could in no way diminish or forget what even they felt was the insult to the messenger, and indeed they could speak of nothing else. This would be a way of saying, as Kafka often suggests about similar dilemmas in his Chinese stories, that other people in the same situation might have had the strength to recover; but they were not other people, only the people they were. What dooms them finally is not Amalia's act or the villagers' craven behaviour but their own traumatized relation to their doom. What the villagers cannot forgive is not the original supposed scandal, but the continuing scandal of the inability to overcome it. They cautiously steal away from the first because they think it might be contagious; they emphatically avoid the second because they know it is the plague.

This perspective allows us, I think, to adjudicate an ancient and stormy debate about the Amalia section of *The Castle* – or, if not to adjudicate, to understand what it means to occupy the wilder interpretative positions, and what other positions there are. The debate began with Max Brod, who thought Sortini's offensive summoning of Amalia was Kafka's analogue for God's asking Abraham to sacrifice Isaac: a request that is outrageous, immoral, and incomprehensible to the merely human mind, but for this very reason a striking measure of the incommensurable will of God. I think this reading misses the cool and complicated tone of Kafka's telling of the story, as well as the depth and scepticism of his engagement with Kierkegaard on the very subject of Abraham and Isaac, but the argument is interesting. We could be required, by our god or by our duty, to commit an act that would be outrageous by ordinary moral standards, and we would need to rise to the occasion rather than consult our old assumptions or an ethics manual. It is a line of thought of this kind that allows Ritchie Robertson, without going to Brod's extremes, to say that Amalia 'is treated with a distinct lack of sympathy' – by Kafka, he means, not by the villagers – and that 'it would seem likely that in asserting her own will against that of the Castle, Amalia is arrogantly rejecting something of potential religious as well as human value'.[2] Erich Heller will have none of this, and nor will Elizabeth Boa or Heinz Politzer. Heller thinks that demons rather than God are behind Sortini's offence, and Boa sees Amalia as making 'the most assertive claim to autonomy in the novel', a bold and imaginative act of resistance to the elaborate mystifications of power, particularly the power of men over women.[3] Politzer goes further. He thinks that Amalia, even before she refused the messenger, while she was still at the festivities around the fire engine, 'read in Sortini's eyes a secret, the secret of the Castle'. We cannot know what she has seen, and neither, *a fortiori*, can anyone in the novel. 'Amalia alone knows what she has seen . . . Having resigned from all her claims to humanity, she has become a holy sister of despair.'[4]

Well, has Amalia turned away from God or seen the heart of darkness? I am sure we can face the alternatives without being so metaphysical, and my own position is closest to Boa's. But I do think we need to respect the ambiguity Kafka has taken such care to establish, because this is precisely where his social vision lies. The multiplication of interpretative possibilities, often a manic or comic or destructive habit in his characters, is also Kafka's way of understanding the intricacy of the world – a form of patience, or what we may think of as an almost unnatural willingness to defer conclusions. Amalia is the solitary opponent of a powerful consensus, and for anyone, inside or outside the novel, who has any sympathy for the consensus, she must seem arrogant and difficult and wrong-headed. She could even, for such persons, be a hero, albeit heroically misguided. Conversely, for anyone who deems the consensus despicable, Amalia must represent the only expression of something like independence to be found anywhere in the novel. She could also, for these persons, be arrogant and difficult and (by local standards) wrong-headed, but these features would be aspects of her virtue. Each of these views is entangled in the other as its refutation, and each rests on textual evidence and (and more or less) defensible assumptions about the world outside the book. I am not proposing that this tangle is itself the final truth about the social world of *The Castle*, since extrapolations are certainly legitimate and often, as I have suggested, irresistible. I am suggesting only that the tangle is where Kafka patiently suspends his enquiry.

What defines Amalia is her difference; what she is different from, it seems, is the whole of her world. But then that world is defined by its difference from Amalia, and we are caught up in a riddle that Kafka shows no sign of solving. I should like to endorse Amalia's revolt, because I admire her virtue and her silence, but in the book she gains nothing except distress for herself and others, and a beleaguered patch of moral high ground. I should like to condemn the family and the village for their weak-kneed subjection to what they take to be the castle's wishes – because of the many known historical cases where a human consensus has called on God or some other unreachable authority to justify the exclusion of other humans from the available forms of social life, and in some instances from life itself. But there is no sign in the book that these people are ready for a less invidious consensus, or that they could live without their submission to the castle's actual and imaginary rule.

At one point Olga says of Amalia that it is not easy to tell whether she is speaking ironically or seriously. 'Mostly she's serious, but she sounds ironic.' K is irritated by this analysis, and says 'Stop interpreting!' (*Laß die Deutungen!*) (*S.* 251; *C.* 266). K's impatience is our clue, I think, a hint from Kafka at the importance of a mode of thought and articulation that would be serious *and* ironic, ironic because it was serious, because in certain complex situations irony is the only adequate form of seriousness. K is also surprised to find in Amalia's family (although not in Amalia herself) the kind of 'unhappy striving' (*S.* 217; *C.* 231–2) he thought was all his own, and could not possibly arise in the village. He associated it with being a foreigner, which Olga, in turn, has associated with having experience: 'You have experience of people, you're a foreigner' (*S.* 211; *C.* 225). One could meditate at length on this run of connections: unhappiness, striving, foreignness, experience. The family has lost what K wants, a place in the world, although of course there is a crucial difference. K came looking for such a place, and he does not just want to settle in the village; he wants access to the castle as well. He wants, to use a perhaps too loaded historical analogy, not only to be assimilated into a community but to be assimilated with advantage, to be both integrated and distinguished. He is too serious, insufficiently ironic, to hang on to a sense of the full complexity of what he wants.

The Castle is unfinished, and there is something problematic about the conclusion Brod says Kafka had in mind: the castle does not recognize K's right to live in the village, yet gives him, on his deathbed, a kind of *de facto* permission. But K already has permission to live in the village from the very start; the trouble is that he does not like the terms, his subordination to the village authorities, and he wants more than that. It may be, as I have suggested, that the sketched resolution is a metaphor for the uncertain home in the world that is all we can aspire to once we have started aspiring, an irony that defines the space between native and immigrant, between different kinds of citizenship, between belonging to a place and just living there – and that may even suggest that 'between' is the place to be, if we can bear it. But we are on firmer ground if we return to a completed chapter in the book, where K finally encounters for himself the social structure that Amalia's story reveals.

K is at last summoned for an audience at the inn with a castle official – not Klamm but someone called Erlanger. It turns out that the man has no direct business with K at all, merely wants to inform him that Frieda is to return to her old job in the bar. But the hour is late, K is sleepy, and he steps meanwhile into the wrong room. But is it the wrong room? We know enough about Kafka's wit and the world of this novel to be certain that a nominally right room could not possibly be the right one. We know too that wrong rooms are often just wrong rooms. The possible crack in the system – is this an invitation to hope as the finest form of despair? – is that a wrong room just might be the right one. There is an official in this room, awake and ready to talk to K, even to discuss his case. His name is Bürgel, and he is the official I mentioned earlier who is astonished that a land surveyor should have no land-surveying to do. Bürgel describes, with exhaustive philosophical patience, as if they were both elsewhere and he was merely offering an example, the precise conditions of their encounter. 'There are sometimes opportunities that are almost not in accord with the general situation, opportunities in which by means of a word, a glance, a sign of trust, more can be achieved than by means of lifelong efforts.' K is almost asleep and is not too interested anyway – he has become too blasé to believe in such opportunities. Bürgel goes on, as if he were some immensely friendly improvement on the doorkeeper and the priest in *The Trial*, 'But, then again, of course, these opportunities are in accord with the general situation in so far as they are never made use of. But why are they never made use of?' (*S.* 315; *C.* 337–8). The scene continues, with Bürgel getting more and more eloquent and K getting more and more dozy, until Bürgel makes an unmistakable, if complicated offer of help.

> And now, Land Surveyor, consider the possibility that through some circumstances or other, in spite of the obstacles already described to you, which are in general quite sufficient, an applicant does nevertheless, in the middle of the night, surprise a secretary who has a certain degree of competence with regard to the given case. . . . You think it cannot happen at all? You are right, it cannot happen at all. But some night – who can vouch for everything? – it *does* happen. . . . It is a situation in which it quickly becomes impossible to refuse a request. . . . The applicant wrings sacrifices from us in the night. . . . (*S.* 323–4; *C.* 346–9)

And, in case the applicant does not get it, the official thus surprised has to explain the whole situation, as Bürgel is doing to K. This is 'the official's hour of travail', Bürgel says. 'But when one has done even that, then, Land Surveyor, all that is essential has been done, then one must resign oneself and wait' (*S.* 325; *C.* 350). Kafka's next words are 'K slept', (*K schlief*), a terse, ironic consummation of the whole scene that recalls certain grimly concise sentences in Flaubert's *Sentimental Education*, a novel Kafka loved greatly.

Erlanger now knocks on the wall, and says K is to come right away. K wakes up and staggers out, dimly aware of what he has missed through sleeping. Bürgel consoles him with the thought I have already paraphrased in relation to the lack of 'strength' of Amalia's family. 'One's physical energies reach only to a certain limit. Who can help the fact that precisely this limit is significant in other ways too? No, nobody can help it. That is how the world itself corrects the deviations in its course and maintains the balance. This is indeed an excellent, time and again unimaginably excellent arrangement, even if in other respects cheerless' (*S.* 326; *C.* 351). Excellent and cheerless – *vorzüglich* and *trostlos*. The castle and the village maintain exactly this arrangment.

Of course, because this a novel by Kafka, we must allow for the possibility that Bürgel's offer of help is false, a game he is playing with K to amuse himself. There would then be no crack at all in the system, only the pretence of a crack, and all wrong rooms would be absolutely wrong rooms. We need to allow for this possibility because its very existence colours Bürgel's speech and alters the irony of K's sleep. But Bürgel's model of social relations, his sense of the world and patterns of advancement, are the same whether his offer of help is genuine or not, and equally instructive in both cases. K may or may not miss a great opportunity in this scene, but he certainly fails, as well he might, to grasp the scope of a system that so easily combines excellence and cheerlessness.

K's sleepiness is weariness of heart as well as physical fatigue. He does not believe in his chances of success with the castle any more than Amalia's family believe in their chances of social reinstatement. The castle and the village have defeated him, or almost defeated him, by teaching him the odds, and getting him to treat the odds as reality. But here is the subtlety of Kafka's desolate social vision, and the most important link between K's quest and Amalia's story. The scene with Bürgel suggests to us, even if only in mockery, that a revolt against local manners or the castle's incursions, indeed any challenge at all to the enormously settled way of this world, is not impossible, or deluded, or doomed, just a very bad bet. It could always succeed in theory, although none has ever succeeded in practice. But then the bet is so bad that it may seem like the merest sanity to give up betting. 'There are opportunities', Bürgel says, 'that are too great to be made use of; there are things that are wrecked on nothing but themselves' (*S.* 327; *C.* 351) – an exquisite way of saying that change is both easy and impossible. Here, as in the case of Amalia's family, the elements of the situation are: an idea of the castle, a community's sense of the world, and a person's (or a set of persons') inability to counteract that view in a sufficiently convincing way. The balance is alterable, as Bürgel suggests, and in no way absolute. But, once a particular balance is in place, the order arrived at will seem inevitable, irremediable, the form of society itself. This is how I read the parable about the Tower of Babel, or rather how I think *The Castle* invites us to revise it. 'If it had been possible to build the Tower of Babel without climbing it, it would have been permitted' (*H.* 31; *G.* 82). If we had climbed the tower, it would no longer have been the Tower of Babel, and the heavens would be full of crows.

Kafka leaves it to his readers to imagine a different world, although of course the sheer delicacy of his understanding of collusion and resistance will help us, if we can overcome the weariness we are likely to share with K. This might be another way of reading the joke about God's hope. There is a kindness of spirit, a sort of utopian streak, in Kafka's despair as we see it in *The Castle*. A political interpretation of 'Plenty of hope for God' could be: no hope in any world I can imagine, but plenty of hope in other worlds, not necessarily imaginary ones.

6

Remains of Light

> Let us agree that literature begins at the moment when literature becomes a question.
>
> (Maurice Blanchot, *De Kafka à Kafka*)

Traces of Kafka are everywhere in modern culture, in forms that go well beyond the notion of influence. There are movies based on *Amerika, The Trial, The Castle,* on Kafka's own doubts and sorrows. A lively animated short film ironically called *Franz Kafka's It's a Wonderful Life* won an Oscar in 1995. Steven Berkoff has staged several ingenious Kafka adaptations, there is a Kafka story by Philip Roth, there are Kafka plays by Alan Bennett. In June 2001, a Philip Glass opera derived from 'In the Penal Colony' opened in New York, having been first performed a year before in Seattle. Kafka haunts the work of Milan Kundera, obviously enough, but also the work of Samuel Beckett, Jorge Luis Borges, Gabriel García Márquez, Harold Pinter, J. M. Coetzee, Kazuo Ishiguro. Kafka's writing is also central to a whole tradition of critical thinking about literature and society, which begins in Walter Benjamin but also includes Hannah Arendt, T. W. Adorno, Maurice Blanchot, Jacques Derrida, Jean-François Lyotard, Gillian Rose, and many others. Slavoj Žižek's *The Sublime Object of Ideology* has a section entitled 'Kafka, Critic of Althusser', which conscripts Kafka for a Lacanian view of the subject and the world, where fantasy is not the opposite of reality but the nefarious agent of whatever reality comes to mean to us. ' "Reality" is a fantasy-construction which enables us to mask the Real of our desire'; and Kafka's universe 'is not a "fantasy-image of social reality" but, on the contrary, the *mise en scène of the fantasy which is at work in the midst of social reality itself'* (emphasis in original).[1]

It would be absurd to try and round up these traces, turn them into a single story about what Kafka has come to mean. We might think a dictionary could help us sort out the legacy a little, though, since not every writer's name becomes an adjective in the way Kafka's has, and we might meditate on the way the form *Kafkaesque* has ousted all the others (*Kafkan, Kafkian, Kafkaish*, and so on). But it turns out that only one Kafka (or at the most two) can be found lingering in the adjective. *Webster's Dictionary* is terse and tautological – 'Of, relating to, or suggestive of Franz Kafka or his writings' – although it does say Kafka is 'Czech-born' rather than simply calling him 'the Austrian writer', as the *Oxford English Dictionary* does. The *OED* is also cautiously tautological – 'Of or relating to the Austrian writer Franz Kafka (1883–1924) or his writing; resembling a state of affairs or a state of mind described by Kafka' – but its instances of usage make the dominant meanings fairly clear. 'Kafkaesque' appears twice in relation to the Moscow Trials, then again in contexts suggesting a powerful bureaucracy, 'a nightmare of blind alleys', an 'atmosphere of despair and horror', and, most interestingly, the 'cruellest of tortures, that of hope'. What the name Kafka mainly suggests is a kind of rigged labyrinth, a labyrinth inseparable from ideas of oppression and power. This vision is an important part of what Kafka's work presents to us, but, as I hope this book has shown, it would be a little sentimental, even self-righteous, to leave it at that, as if we had no stake in the labyrinth ourselves, or did not know how we had got lost there.

Kafka is not only a writer and a name, he is something like a memory we scarcely know we have. He himself offers a miniature theory of this kind of trace or existence. In a notebook he writes the following mundane sentence, 'But then he returned to his work, just as though nothing had happened', and comments, 'This is a remark we are familiar with from a vague profusion of old stories, although perhaps it does not occur in any one of them' (*H.* 40; *G.* 98). How can this non-occurring remark, or this type of remark, seem so familiar? Well, we may think of old films and other fictions as well as Kafka's old stories: all the absolutely characteristic gestures that Sherlock Holmes did not actually make, the famous lines from *Casablanca* that are spoken only in cultural memory, and not in the film. Benjamin cites the comment in relation to a quite different phrase from the one Kafka offers, assuming it applies quite generally to any sedimented, habit-haunted piece of language. Certain words or sets of words, like certain sensations, produce the effect of quotation, of *déjà vu* or *déjà lu*, although we cannot place them exactly, and may never have encountered them before – indeed, as Kafka suggests, they may not have been present in any of the places where we could have encountered them. The quotation effect is real, nevertheless. It is as if culture itself were speaking to us, reminding us of our lateness, and of all the relays of knowledge that make up what we think we know – and what we do know. We feel we have been here before, when we have only been somewhere like this, and when 'here' is a name for several overlapping territories. The error, if it is one, concentrates and simplifies the original, like a tiny myth. We think we know Kafka better than we do, but we cannot undo the knowledge we think we have. That is a tribute to his work, and a danger for it. He has become part of our language. We speak Kafka, and, like most native speakers, are not always aware of the principles of our idiom.

We can illustrate Kafka's traces, of course, and the quickest way of doing that is perhaps to call up those passages in Kafka that seem so clearly to have been written by one of his successors. The old couple who are taken out in a wheelbarrow every day, in order to wait by the roadside for an official who will never stop for them – we saw them somewhere in Beckett, did we not, rather than in *The Castle*? When García Márquez describes his indebtedness to 'The Metamorphosis', his schooling at its tone of determined unsurprise, it seems as if Kafka might have invented magic realism itself. When we read of the adherents of the old Commandant of 'In the Penal Colony' who are no longer allowed to bear any name, we seem to have entered the secret world of Thomas Pynchon, or Don DeLillo, or Umberto Eco. 'You misinterpret everything, even silence' – surely that comes from a Pinter play, and not, again, from *The Castle* (*S.* 101; *C.* 105). The great board that shows the names of those accepted by the Nature Theatre of Oklahoma in *Amerika* appears in only slightly altered form in Ishiguro's *The Unconsoled*. The idea of a person looking different when he arrives in a village from when he leaves, different before and after he has had a drink, different when asleep and when awake, different when alone and when in conversation – are these not the perceptions of the endlessly precise Funes the Memorious, in Borges's story of that name, rather than various perspectives on the official Klamm, yet again in *The Castle*?

But the traces do not add up to single afterlife for Kafka, and there is no reason why they should. Rather than try to summarize his legacy, or even to evoke its full range, I want in conclusion to look at its intensity, its sheer continuing vitality, in three very different modes: a film, a body of philosophical work, an opera.

The most famous image in Orson Welles's 1963 film of *The Trial* is the last one, a vast mushroom cloud locating us immediately in the aftermath of Hiroshima and Nagasaki. In the film as in the novel Joseph K's executioners take him to a disused quarry, and pass a knife back and forth in front of his eyes, inviting him to take it and finish the job himself. In both cases he refuses the invitation, in the film in so many words. But then in the novel one of the executioners drives the knife into K's heart and turns it there twice. In the film both men scamper away, tossing a lighted bundle of dynamite back into the quarry as they go. There is the expected explosion, in which K presumably dies, but then the clouds keep mounting, in quantities well beyond anything that dynamite could do, and finally shape themselves into that radioactive figure we know so well. In interviews Welles later said he did not have this familiar image in mind – 'I really didn't mean that big atom-bomb thing'[2] – but he seems to have been resisting its obviousness rather than its actual meaning, and he did say he felt he needed 'to move into high gear' at that moment of the film. 'I don't want to say that my ending was good, but it was the only solution'.[3]

The logic of the move is quite clear. Dynamite is not an atom bomb, but the explosion affords a link between this catastrophic conclusion and what has gone before. One madness leads to another, Welles is saying, or, more precisely, if you think the world is mad there is no limit to what you can do. Ivan Karamazov's 'Everything is permitted' was a reflection of a lost morality. Welles's reading of Kafka makes such permission a matter of lost sanity. Well, not just lost: comprehensively ruined, made unavailable. 'That's the conspiracy', Welles's K says in one of his moments of illumination. 'To persuade us all that the whole world is crazy. Formless, meaningless, absurd . . . Does that sentence the entire universe to lunacy?' This would not be a conspiracy in the ordinary sense, a focused, coordinated plan of the kind terrorists and paranoids dream of. It would be a kind of dedication to arbitrariness and disorder to which almost anything could contribute, not only anarchy and prejudice and apathy and confusion but even extreme forms of order if they were incoherent or violent enough in their goals. It is not at all obvious how such dedication could end once it has started, and that, we may imagine, is Welles's point.

How does Welles get Kafka's text to tell this story, which seems closer to the mood of *The Castle* than to that of *The Trial*? It seems at first sight that he simply makes K the innocent victim of a huge and capricious social machine, metaphorically represented in the vast bank of computers shown at the office where K works. Many of the most memorable images in the film strongly reinforce this effect: a long tracking shot through row upon row of busy typists in a kind of hangar that seems to extend into infinity; endless corridors and corners of deserted public buildings; the vacant lots of some archetypical twentieth-century city, always under cheaply funded construction; mountains of dog-eared and abandoned documents; faces distorted to monstrosity by a fish-eye lens; low-angle shots that turn ordinary people into giants, and ordinary rooms into Expressionist nightmares. The very use of black and white for the film points in the same direction, as if Welles had wanted to make a sort of metaphysical *film noir*, Joseph K meets James M. Cain. The casting of Anthony Perkins is important too, since he projects such a perfectly jittery, wounded helplessness throughout, even when (especially when) he is trying to take control of things. And what man in the 1960s would not be helpless if he was distracted by actresses like Jeanne Moreau,

Elsa Martinelli, and Romy Schneider? Welles understood the curious vulnerability towards women, along with the willingness to use and abuse them, that runs through all of Kafka's fiction, and translated it into the language of mid-century film mythology: his K is tempted and bewildered not by the attractive but unprepossessing Friedas and Pepis and Lenis of the fiction but by three of the most troubling and imperious actresses of the time.

Welles's K is not innocent, though. He is victimized, but that is not the same thing. Perkins's very nervousness, especially at the beginning of the film, means he cannot just be the beleaguered Everyman Welles sometimes (but only sometimes) seems to be after. What is K accused of? We do not know, either in the film or the novel. An arrest under such circumstances is a quite flagrant violation of anything we might think of as civil or indeed human rights. But, in Welles as in Kafka, there is a cruel, devastating twist. If the court is wrong to accuse you without naming the crime, you must be wrong, for the very same reason, to proclaim your innocence. K's confusion, his failure even to see the rights he should be standing up for, his lamentable willingness to play the court's games of influence, insinuation, and reckless misinterpretation, are all as much part of the world's madness as the court's own invasion of privacy is. This does not make K guilty, of course – or it makes him guilty only of being an indispensable part of the very conspiracy he is denouncing. To use Welles's own phrasing, 'He is not guilty as accused, but he is guilty all the same. He belongs to a guilty society . . .'.[4]

In this light the extraordinary visual atmosphere of the film begins to change, or double, its meaning. We need to remember that *The Trial* looks, above all, like a film by Orson Welles: like *The Magnificent Ambersons*, or *Othello*, or *Touch of Evil*, or *The Lady from Shanghai*, none of which is based on a text by Kafka. Welles's world is one of shadows and low ceilings, of friezelike mortuary processions, of decaying detectives and fortune-tellers, of impenetrable crimes and elaborately cracked mirrors. I do not want to suggest this is already the world of Kafka, in advance of Welles's making *The Trial*. I do want to suggest that Kafka and Welles found each other in this film. *The Trial* does not eclipse other visual analogues or actualizations of Kafka's work, but it is unmistakably the most powerful one so far, so that, if we try to *see* Kafka, we are likely to see Welles. Welles seems to have filmed, made visual, the dwarfing of human life that recurs in Kafka, found unforgettable locations for all the echoing, airless spaces we find in his fiction. Much of the film was shot in the Gare d'Orsay in Paris, after it had ceased operating as a railway station and before it became a museum. 'The thing that gave it a particular force', Welles said, 'is that it is not only a very large place to work in, and a very beautiful place to photograph, but that it is full of sorrow – the kind of sorrow that accumulates in a railway station where people wait . . . I know this sounds terribly mystical, but really a railway station is a haunted place.'[5]

Conversely, Welles discovered in Kafka something he had long been looking for: a universe in which neither innocence nor guilt had to be denied, or could be denied. 'I've had recurring nightmares of guilt all my life,' Welles said, adding that *The Trial* was 'the most autobiographical movie that I've ever made, the *only* one that's really close to me' (emphasis in original).[6] So that what we see in the amazing and ominous interiors of this film is not only a world ganging up on the unfortunate K, literally hanging over him, but a picture of his mind turned inside out, a world made exactly in the image of his fears. That these two worlds are not incompatible, that indeed there is only one world, made up out of the (usually) unholy conflation of the two perspectives, is one of Kafka's great insights, as I have already suggested. Welles's mushroom cloud is a slightly too blustery underlining of this insight.

Readings of Kafka are crucial to the work of the English philosopher Gillian Rose, who died, far too early, in 1995. She is very drawn to those interpretations of the story 'Before the Law' that see it as a fable about passivity. The man from the country was not deceived by the doorkeeper, these commentaries say; he merely timidly obeyed him, failed to understand that disobedience was among his options. Perhaps the man was punished, Rose says in *Judaism and Modernity*, glossing Benjamin's suggestion that Kafka's characters have lost the scriptures, 'not because he has lost access to the doorway of the Law, to learning, but because of his refusal to keep his promise to life, to struggle with the doorman who seems to bar access to the Law'. Benjamin, Rose says, 'does not raise the possibility that Joseph K might be guilty (as Orson Welles implies in his film of *The Trial*)'.[7] The doorman seems to bar access; and may actually bar it. We do not know what the result of the man's struggle would have been, because he does not struggle. In this light the story perfectly reflects the crisis of authority that Rose finds central to the very notion of modernity. To put the matter far too simply, if an authority is legitimate, we may obey it without qualms; if it is illegitimate, we may seek to overthrow it. But what if we do not know how legitimate it is, or what our criteria for legitimacy are? And what if these questions are themselves endless?

'The more liberal Judaism becomes', Rose writes in *Love's Work*, 'the less the orientation by . . . the law, and the greater the emphasis on individual faith in God'. She quotes a friend as saying that 'An Orthodox Jew does not have to worry about whether he believes in God or not. As long as he observes the law'. This brings to her mind 'the notoriously inscrutable Midrash: "Would that they would forsake Me, but obey my Torah".'[8] God himself would be extremely Orthodox in this representation, disapproving of 'individual faith' even if it brought His worshippers closer to Him, or perhaps for that very reason. Well, He would be if we take Him literally. But Midrash is commentary, not revelation, and God Himself is not present in this sentence as He was in His instructions to Moses. The Rabbis picture God as expressing His curious wish; the inscrutable formulation is a miniature story, a performance, and who knows what reserves of irony and mockery lurk in it. Perhaps God means to suggest a redress of balance, the correction of an excessive inwardness, rather than a total dependence on the law and an actual forsaking of Himself. Or perhaps He means the reverse, and is working in the mode of parody. His children have already forsaken Him, and have nothing but their blind obedience to the law. Or, more drastically, He thinks the separation of Himself and the law is itself erroneous, and wants to make this clear through an extravagant appearance of abnegation. Needless to say, I am not suggesting we can settle these intricate matters, only that all interpretations will dramatize a difficult or ambiguous relation with authority, and an uncertainty about where that authority is to be located. 'Authority in crisis', Rose writes in *Mourning Becomes the Law*, 'requires political risk *greater* than that required in traditional society' (emphasis in original).[9] And not just political risk, unless we take politics in its very broadest sense. The risk is whatever risk the man from the country would not or could not take.

Conflating Weber and Benjamin, Rose often thinks of this world of risk and crisis as a world shaken by Protestantism, in which a melancholy inner life either fails to reach out to the realm of action or abandons that realm to its most ruthless inhabitants – or both. Protestants, in this view, have lost their 'interest in salvation', but an 'anxiety of salvation persists'[10] – and in this sense who could be more of a Protestant than Kafka? Protestantism, in a phrase of Benjamin's which Rose cites, is marked by 'the awareness of being alone with one's God'[11] – precisely what God seems not to want in the Midrash evoked above. In a posthumous work called *Paradiso*, Rose evokes a friend's failure to understand that 'modernity is Protestant, not humanistic; it is founded on Luther's "bondage of the will" not on Erasmus's "freedom of the will", on heteronomy not on autonomy. Kant not Descartes . . .'.[12] To be a Protestant, for Rose, is to be freed from an old order while still seeking for a new one, and perhaps to have lost God in the process. To be a dogmatic Protestant is to be sure you have found the new order and to be certain that your God is the only one. The crisis of authority necessarily includes excessive denials of the crisis.

Rose sometimes spells 'protestant' with a small p, to mark a recurring tendency within quite different traditions. In *Love's Work*, for example, she attacks New Age spirituality as a kind of exitless cruelty to the self, 'the most remorseless protestantism' – because all it does is allow people to blame themselves for their own illness. More ambiguously, she describes dyslexia and the inability to read as 'a blind protestantism, an unconscious rebellion, against the law, the tradition of the fathers, and against the precipitous fortress of the family'. The rebellion might be necessary, but the mode is self-damaging. Elsewhere, though, a group of protestants (small p but clearly ethnic if not religious) at 'an ordinary English wedding' are said to be 'weightless, redeemed beings' compared with a heavy and sorrowful community of Hasidic Jews living in the same neighbourhood.[13] These instances – dogma, rebellion, redemption – are all responses, or dreamed responses, to the shaken, questionable institutions of the law. They belong to the world of what Rose calls, in the title of another book, *The Broken Middle*.

Rose wants us to 'risk comprehension of the broken middle', the 'ancient and broken heart of modernity',[14] and to do this is to restore reason, not to abandon it. 'The authority of reason', she says, 'is risk. Reason, the critical criterion, is for ever without ground.'[15] Without permanent or static ground, she means, without end or beginning. She takes to heart Benjamin's paradoxical view of Kafka's work as ultimately possessing, more than anything else, 'the purity and beauty of a failure'. 'One is tempted to say,' Benjamin continues, 'once he was certain of eventual failure, everything worked out for him *en route* as in a dream'.[16] Rose would add, I think, that Kafka was not even certain of failure, that risk never left him. Reading Brod's account of God's bad moods and the abundance of hope for God if not for us, Rose insists on Kafka's smile as he makes the remark. 'God possesses our hope, as it were,' Rose says. 'We are not only absent to ourselves in hope, but even this hope is absent to us.' But the smile couples God's bad humour and our hopelessness into something else: 'the passionate good humour of the utterer and the utterance, beyond hope or hopelessness.'[17] Beyond success or failure too. If only he knew it, risk, understood as reason rather than wild recklessness or a secretly rigged game, is all the authority the man from the country needs.

Philip Glass's *In the Penal Colony*, which he informally calls a 'pocket opera', is more ceremoniously known as a 'music-theatre work'. It is scored for two singing parts, the officer (bass-baritone) and the traveller (tenor), and for string quintet (two violins, viola, cello, and double bass). There is an extensive speaking part for Franz Kafka, reciting hair-raising chunks from his diaries and letters, and occasionally joining in the action he is manifestly imagining: 'The tremendous world I have in my head', he says more than once. 'But how to free myself and free it without being torn to pieces.'[18] There are also two acting but non-speaking parts for the condemned man and the soldier who guards him. The libretto is by Rudolph Wurlitzer.

The music is minimal and lucid, slightly repetitive, discreetly lyrical in the cool, high modernist manner. It is clear that the work concerns Kafka and writing as much as it does justice and the colony, and the Seattle/New York production, although entirely persuasive, had a slightly worried air about it, as if some residual unpersuaded dissent lurked in the mind of the director JoAnne Akalaitis. A clue to the worry may lie in Akalaitis's programme note, where she says she suspects the piece 'may be about the agony of writing, creation, the way things fall apart and the danger of change'. She adds, quite strikingly, that 'Kafka's story is not about capital punishment'. She means it is not *only* about capital punishment, that its main interest, in 1914 or 2001, is not topical, but I am not sure the topical is such a threat or entirely irrelevant. It is a fallacy to think that a writer like Kafka must be concerned with enduring 'big' subjects rather than matters of concern to newspapers, or, worse, that 'the agony of writing' is a real subject while contemporary public events are not. These are not alternatives; their apparent opposition is itself a form of cultural anxiety. The opera is about writing, of course, and the presence of Kafka on the stage guarantees this, but the word 'execution' occurs again and again in the text of Glass's work ('I accepted the invitation to the execution out of courtesy', the traveller sings, and asks whether the new Commandant will be attending 'the execution',[19] and there is no way of shrinking capital punishment into a mere metaphor. There may also be a trace, even in this production and even in 2001, of the reaction that has accompanied 'In the Penal Colony' and other Kafka stories from the moment of their first reading, 'a shielding hand over the eyes or an averted gaze', as Mark Anderson says, a shift of attention 'away from the first and literal level of the story ... in an attempt to get behind or beyond this level and understand its "deeper" significance'.[20] The only way beyond, I am afraid, assuming we want to get there, is through the literal.

The New York programme says the penal colony is 'off the coast of Africa'. There are no geographical indications in the libretto, and no historical indications beyond the fact that the officer sings of his homeland, and tells the traveller that the prisoner does not understand 'their' language. In Kafka's text the language the prisoner does not understand is said to be French, and the obvious association for Kafka himself and for many others would be Devil's Island, close to Cayenne, internationally famous because of Alfred Dreyfus's incarceration there from 1894 to 1899. But Kafka may also have been thinking of Russian penal colonies, which he knew about from reading Dostoyevsky, and perhaps Chekhov, who visited Sakhalin in 1890 and wrote a book about it. The mention of Africa for the opera, and the presence in the New York production of a black American actor and singer (the soldier and the officer, although the prisoner is white), suggests a generically European colony (English, French, German, Belgian), and the conjunction of these various imperial enterprises broadens the idea without losing any of its key historical aspects. The libretto emphasizes the homeland in a way that the story does not, moving from a conversation about the military uniforms, surely too heavy for the tropics, the traveller thinks, into an overtly lyrical memory. 'But they represent our homeland,' the officer sings. 'And I'm sure you agree: we must never forget our homeland. Where would we be? Who would we be? If we forget where we come from?' The officer also evokes 'that precious land that sent us here. The land that one day will call us back.'[21] This is to stress the colonizing enterprise, and to suggest a continuity between punishments at home and abroad, while Kafka seems to be more interested in the peculiar penal life of *this* colony, inviting us to thoughts of empire by extrapolation rather than unbroken historical realism. But both opera and story focus our attention on the conjunction of colony and punishment, on versions of distance and extreme behaviour that on inspection turn out to be closer and more familiar than we may have thought, like the Tibetan village in Kafka's letter to Milena. How could they be far?

And here a curious shift occurs in the opera, entirely faithful to one strand of Kafka's thought, but dramatically unbalanced if we think of the eerie coolness of the overall tone of the story. Kafka's presence on stage makes clear his writing agony, and in itself is a comment on the horror of such imaginings. But he talks, he does not sing, and the medium makes all the difference. The officer in the story has his passionate moments, when he is carried away by the memory of the ruthless and radiant old days, but what is scary about him is his characteristic pre-Eichmann calm. The officer in the opera *is* his passionate moments, the score at these points abandons its minimalism for accents of expansive rapture, and there is nothing a talking Kafka can do to put these sounds and images back into the privacy of nightmare. Most of the words of the libretto are already in the story, but the repetitions are not, and of course the music has all kinds of irresistible meanings of its own. About the illumination of the sixth hour, in previous executions, the officer sings:

> Even the least of men is now enlightened.
> It starts around the eyes and from there it spreads.
> A look that might seduce you,
> Tempt you, into joining him.
> Yes, joining him under the harrow.
> Yes, joining him under the harrow.[22]

The words name the seduction but the music enacts it, and it is aimed directly at us. We cannot join an imaginary prisoner under the harrow, of course, least of all one who exists only in (fictional) memory, but we can join the officer in his enthusiasm, and it is very hard not to. The same danger recurs a little later, when the officer sings again about the old executions:

> Then came the sixth hour!
> Everyone wanted to see his face.
> The old commander ordered that children be given preference.
> I would stand close with a child in each hand.
> How deeply we took in the transfigured expression from the tortured face.
> How intensely the tiny cheeks basked in the glow of justice, attained at last and then already fading.[23]

Here Wurlitzer has added virtually nothing to Kafka. But Glass has added all the lyrical authority he can muster. What Kafka fears and describes Glass gets a voice to sing and a quintet to play. We can see why Akalaitis and even Glass himself might want to retreat from the immediacy (and beauty) of these horrors into something more generalized like the agony of writing. In an earlier chapter I suggested that, unlikely and unappealing as it may seem, we do share the disappointment and the solitude of the officer. Until I saw the Glass opera I had not imagined we could actually be invited to share his conviction, his passionate intensity, to borrow an all too relevant phrase from Yeats.[24] The opera as a whole does not issue this invitation, far from it. But its finest moments do, and they are the ones that send us reeling from the theatre, almost nostalgic for the banality of evil. There is nothing banal about the idea of evil Glass has found in Kafka, or in the phrases I have already quoted from one of Kafka's letters: 'this descent to the dark powers, this unchaining of spirits bound by nature, these questionable embraces and whatever else goes on down there, that one knows no more about up here, when one writes stories in the sunlight.' Down there is where you find those tiny cheeks basking in the justice of torture.

Kafka's stories and novels are often funny but none of them is written in the sunlight. Their chief project, as I have suggested, is to represent the vain attempt to tame extremes, to recapture the ordinary – along with the ghastly revenge of the ordinary, on the few occasions when it allows itself to be recaptured. But this project has a corollary. The devil is master of the ordinary and the extraordinary; he knows how to use all the registers. The officer of 'In the Penal Colony' both announces and surpasses Eichmann, because he brings ordinary virtues to his extraordinary calling, and because he is not just obeying orders. He believes in his orders; they are his life. When he selects his own sentence and submits to the machine, we realize that the sentences in this colony are really idealizing commandments: 'Be Just!' 'Honour thy Superiors!' These are instructions that go well beyond any particular infringement. The officer sees all this, and he is right to condemn himself. He is doubly guilty, for obeying hideous orders and for believing in them, and his being right in his judgement does not redeem him from the judgement. It does, however, leave us in a quandary, precisely because the devil has mixed up the officer's virtues with his crimes. In any writer other than Kafka it would be easier to deny our kinship with the officer. Here we have to go beyond denial (and endorsement), and explore the darkness of the relation. We need to accept the man's 'questionable embrace' and also walk away. There are many ways of acting on the instruction to be just, not necessarily dishonourable because they are different from each other. Do we know how to distinguish between admirable devotions and murderous ends, between rigour and cruelty, between loyalty and madness? The historical record is not encouraging, but, as Kafka keeps showing us, there are truths to be glimpsed in the light on the grimacing faces.

Notes

CHAPTER 1. A COMMON CONFUSION

1. *The Selected Poetry of Rainer Maria Rilke*, ed. and trans. Stephen Mitchell (New York: Vintage, 1989), 150, 151.
2. Peter Stern, revised by Sheila Stern, 'Elegy One', in *Rilke's Duino Elegies*, ed. Roger Paulin and Peter Hutchinson (London: Duckworth, 1996), 5.
3. Erich Heller, *The Disinherited Mind* (New York: Harcourt Brace Jovanovich, 1975), 211.

CHAPTER 2. THE STUDENT OF PRAGUE

1. Cited by Jost Schillemeit in his Afterword to Franz Kafka, *Der Verschollene* (Frankfurt: Fischer, 1993), 328.
2. *Das Kafka-Buch*, ed. Heinz Politzer (Frankfurt: Fischer, 1965), 216 (=Letter, 5 July 1922).
3. Robert Musil, *Der Mann ohne Eigenschaften* (Hamburg: Rowohlt, 1970), 33–4.
4. Ibid. 170.
5. Robert Musil, *Tagebücher*, ed. Adolf Frisé, 2 vols. (Hamburg: Rowohlt, 1976), i. 354.
6. Musil, *Der Mann ohne Eigenschaften*, 32.
7. Angelo Maria Ripellino, *Magic Prague*, trans. David Newton Marinelli, ed. Michael Henry Heim (London: Picador, 1995).
8. Gustav Janouch, *Conversations with Kafka*, trans. Goronwy Rees (New York: New Directions, 1971), 80.
9. Max Brod, *Franz Kafka: A Biography*, trans. G. Humphreys Roberts and Richard Winston (New York: Da Capo, 1995), 75.
10. Ibid. 3.
11. Paul de Man, *Wartime Journalism 1939–1943*, ed. Werner

Hamacher, Neil Hertz, and Thomas Keenan (Lincoln, Neb.: University of Nebraska Press, 1988), 45.

12. Walter Benjamin, *Illuminations*, trans. Harry Zohn (New York: Schocken, 1969), 261.
13. Robert Alter, 'Jewish Dreams and Nightmares', in *What Is Jewish Literature?*, ed. Hana Wirth-Nesher (Philadelphia: Jewish Publication Society, 1994), 61.
14. Ibid. 62.
15. Ibid. 59, 64.
16. *Benjamin über Kafka*, ed. Hermann Schweppenhäuser (Frankfurt: Suhrkamp, 1981), 91.
17. Benjamin, *Illuminations*, 134.
18. Thomas Hardy, 'In Tenebris II', in *Complete Poems* (London: Macmillan, 1981), 168.
19. Søren Kierkegaard, *Fear and Trembling*, trans. Alastair Hannay (London: Penguin, 1985), 45–6

CHAPTER 3. THE TAMING OF SURPRISE

1. Hannah Arendt, *Eichmann in Jerusalem: A Report on the Banality of Evil* (New York: Viking, 1964).
2. Pietro Citati, *Kafka*, trans. Raymond Rosenthal (New York: Knopf, 1989), 77.
3. Danièle Huillet and Jean-Marie Straub, *Klassenverhältnisse*, ed. Wolfram Schütte (Frankfurt: Fischer, 1984), 58.
4. Stanley Corngold, *Franz Kafka: The Necessity of Form* (Ithaca, NY: Cornell University Press, 1988), 223.
5. J. P. Stern, *Hitler: The Führer and the People* (London: Fontana, 1990), 114.
6. Roland Barthes, *The Rustle of Language*, trans. Richard Howard (Oxford: Blackwell), 141–8.
7. Ludwig Wittgenstein, *Tractatus Logic-Philosophicus*, trans. C. K. Ogden (London: Routledge, 1981), 31.
8. Ludwig Wittgenstein, *Philosophical Investigations*, trans. G. E. M. Anscombe (Oxford: Blackwell, 1967), 37.
9. Cited by Thomas Mann, in *The Castle*, trans. Willa and Edwin Muir (New York: Schocken, 1995), p. xxxix.

CHAPTER 4. MEMORIES OF JUSTICE

1. Paul de Man, *Blindness and Insight* (Minneapolis: University of Minnesota Press, 1983), 141.

2. Michel Foucault, *Discipline and Punish*, trans. Alan Sheridan (London: Penguin, 1991), 3–6.
3. Matt. 11: 12.
4. Philip Roth, *Portnoy's Complaint* (New York: Random House, 1969).

CHAPTER 5. SLEEP AND SOCIETY

1. Avital Ronell, 'Doing Kafka in *The Castle*', in *Kafka and the Contemporary Critical Performance*, ed. Alan Udoff (Bloomington, Ind.: Indiana University Press, 1987), 217, 220.
2. Ritchie Robertson, *Kafka: Judaism, Politics, and Literature* (Oxford: Oxford University Press, 1985), 261, 260.
3. Elizabeth Boa, *Kafka: Gender, Class, and Race in the Letters and Fiction* (Oxford: Clarendon Press, 1996), 248.
4. Heinz Politzer, *Franz Kafka: Parable and Paradox* (Ithaca, NY: Cornell University Press, 1962), 271, 272.

CHAPTER 6. REMAINS OF LIGHT

1. Slavoj Žižek, *The Sublime Object of Ideology* (London: Verso), 45, 36.
2. Orson Welles and Peter Bogdanovich, *This Is Orson Welles* (NewYork: HarperCollins, 1992), 275
3. *Perspectives on Orson Welles*, ed. Morris Beja (New York: G. K. Hall, 1995), 37
4. Ibid. 37
5. Welles and Bogdanovich, *This Is Orson Welles*, 247
6. Ibid. 283.
7. Gillian Rose, *Judaism and Modernity* (Oxford: Blackwell, 1993), 200.
8. Gillian Rose, *Love's Work* (New York: Schocken, 1996), 22–3, 23–4.
9. Gillian Rose, *Mourning Becomes the Law* (Cambridge: Cambridge University Press, 1996), 83.
10. Rose, *Judaism and Modernity*, 180.
11. Ibid. 204.
12. Gillian Rose, *Paradiso* (London: Menard Press, 1999), 20.
13. Rose, *Love's Work*, 105, 37, 44–5.
14. Gillian Rose, *The Broken Middle* (Oxford: Blackwell, 1992), 308–10.
15. Rose, *Love's Work*, 127–8.
16. Walter Benjamin, *Illuminations*, trans. Harry Zohn (New York: Schocken, 1969), 145.
17. Rose, *The Broken Middle*, 75–6.

18. *In the Penal Colony: The Libretto* (New York: Dunvagen Music Publishers, 2000), 1, 18.
19. Ibid. 3, 11.
20. Mark Anderson, *Kafka's Clothes* (Oxford: Oxford University Press, 1992), 174.
21. *In the Penal Colony: The Libretto*, 5.
22. Ibid. 14.
23. Ibid. 18.
24. Cf. Elizabeth Boa (*Kafka: Gender, Class, and Race in the Letters and Fiction* (Oxford: Clarendon Press, 1996), 136, where the traveller is compared to the best who 'lack all conviction' and the officer to the worst who are 'full of passionate intensity'. I read Ms Boa's book after I had written the sentence borrowing Yeats's phrase, but she was plainly the first to make the historical connection.

Select Bibliography

WORKS BY FRANZ KAFKA

Major works in German

Amerika (Frankfurt: Fischer, 1953); also published as *Der Verschollene* (Frankfurt: Fischer, 1993).
Beschreibung eines Kampfes (Frankfurt: Fischer, 1954).
Briefe 1902–1924 (Frankfurt: Fischer, 1958).
Briefe an Felice (Munich: Hanser, 1969).
Briefe an Milena (Frankfurt: Fischer, 1952, 1986).
Hochzeitsvorbereitungen auf dem Lande (Frankfurt: Fischer, 1953, 1983).
Der Proceß (Frankfurt: Fischer, 1950, 1993).
Sämtliche Erzählungen (Frankfurt: Fischer, 1952, 1970).
Das Schloß (Frankfurt: Fischer, 1951, 1994).
Tagebücher 1910–1923 (Frankfurt: Fischer, 1951, 1973).

Major works in English

America, trans. Willa and Edwin Muir (London: Secker & Warburg, 1973); also known as *The Man Who Disappeared*, trans. Michael Hofmann (London: Penguin, 1996).
The Castle, trans. Willa and Edwin Muir (New York: Schocken, 1995).
The Castle, trans. J. A. Underwood (London: Penguin, 1997).
The Castle, trans. Mark Harman (New York: Schocken, 1998).
The Complete Stories, ed. Nahum N. Glatzer (New York: Schocken, 1971).
Diaries 1910–1923, trans. Joseph Kresh and Martin Greenberg (London: Penguin, 1982).
Letters to Felice, trans. James Stern and Elizabeth Duckworth (London: Secker & Warburg, 1974).
Letters to Milena, trans. Tania and James Stern (London: Secker & Warburg, 1953).

The Trial, trans. Willa and Edwin Muir (New York: Schocken, 1995).
The Trial, trans. Idris Parry (London: Penguin, 1994).
The Trial, trans. Breon Mitchell (New York: Schocken, 1998).

BIOGRAPHY

Brod, Max, *Franz Kafka*, trans. G. Humphreys Roberts and Richard Winston (New York: Da Capo, 1995).
Citati, Pietro, *Kafka*, trans. Raymond Rosenthal (Secker & Warburg, 1990).
Hayman, Ronald, *A Biography of Franz Kafka* (London: Weidenfeld & Nicolson, 1981).
Janouch, Gustav, *Conversations with Kafka*, trans. Goronwy Rees (New York: New Directions, 1971).
Karl, F. R., *Franz Kafka* (Boston: Ticknor & Fields, 1991).
Northey, Anthony, *Kafka's Relatives: Their Lives and his Writing* (New Haven: Yale University Press, 1991).
Pawel, Ernst, *The Nightmare of Reason: A Life of Franz Kafka* (London: Harvill, 1984).
Unseld, Joachim, *Franz Kafka: A Writer's Life*, trans. Paul F. Dvorak (Riverside: Ariadne, 1994).

CRITICISM AND CONTEXTS

This is a tiny selection from a vast empire of books. I have concentrated on the ones I found most useful or enlightening, and I have mainly (but not exclusively) listed works in English.

Adorno, Theodor W., *Prisms*, trans. Samuel Weber and Shierry Weber (Cambridge, Mass.: MIT Press, 1983).
Alter, Robert, *Necessary Angels* (Cambridge, Mass.: Harvard University Press, 1991).
Anders, Günther, *Kafka pro et contra*, trans. A. Steer and A. K. Thorlby (London: Bowes & Bowes, 1960).
Anderson, Mark (ed.), *Reading Kafka* (New York: Schocken, 1989).
—— *Kafka's Clothes* (Oxford: Oxford University Press, 1992).
Arendt, Hannah, *Between Past and Future* (New York: Viking, 1961).
Beißner, Friedrich, *Der Erzähler Franz Kafka* (Stuttgart: Wohlhammer, 1952).
—— *Der Dichter Franz Kafka* (Stuttgart: Wohlhammer, 1958).
Benjamin, Walter, *Illuminations*, trans. Harry Zohn (New York: Schocken, 1969).
Binder, Hartmut, *Kafka-Kommentar* (Munich: Winkler, 1976).

Blanchot, Maurice, *The Sirens' Song: Selected Essays*, trans. Sacha Rabinovitch (Brighton: Harvester 1982).

Boa, Elizabeth, *Kafka: Gender, Class, and Race in the Letters and Fictions* (Oxford: Clarendon Press, 1996).

Borges, Jorge Luis, 'Kafka and his Precursors' and 'Funes the Memorious', in *Labyrinths*, trans. Donald A. Yates and James E. Irby (New York: New Directions, 1962).

Canetti, Elias, *Kafka's Other Trial*, trans. Christopher Middleton (London: Penguin, 1983).

Corngold, Stanley, *Franz Kafka: The Necessity of Form* (Ithaca, NY: Cornell University Press, 1988).

Deleuze, Gilles, and Guattari, Felix, *Toward a Minor Literature*, trans. Dana Polan (Minneapolis: University of Minnesota Press, 1986).

Dowden, Stephen, *Kafka's Castle* (Columbia, SC: Camden House, 1995).

Emrich, Wilhelm, *Franz Kakfa*, trans. Sheema Zeben Buehne (New York: Ungar, 1968).

Gilman, Sander L, *Franz Kafka: The Jewish Patient* (New York: Routledge, 1995).

Gray, Ronald, *Kafka's Castle* (Cambridge: Cambridge University Press, 1956).

—— *Franz Kafka* (Cambridge: Cambridge University Press, 1973).

Gray, R. T., *Constructive Deconstruction* (Tübingen: Niemeyer, 1987).

Grözinger, K. E., *Kafka and the Kabbalah*, trans. Susan Hecker Ray (New York: Continuum, 1994).

Heidsieck, A., *The Intellectual Contexts of K's Fiction* (Columbia, SC: Camden House, 1994).

Heller, Erich, *Franz Kafka* (London: Fontana, 1974).

—— *The Disinherited Mind* (New York: Harcourt Brace Jovanovich, 1975).

Koelb, Clayton, *Kafka's Rhetoric* (Ithaca, NY: Cornell University Press, 1989).

Kundera, Milan, *The Art of the Novel*, trans. Linda Asher (London: Faber, 1988).

—— *Testaments Betrayed*, trans. Linda Asher (London: Faber, 1995).

Pascal, Roy, *Kafka's Narrators* (Cambridge: Cambridge University Press, 1982).

Pasley, Malcolm, *Die Schrift ist unveränderlich* (Frankfurt: Fischer, 1995).

Politzer, Heinz, *Franz Kafka: Parable and Paradox* (Ithaca, NY: Cornell University Press, 1962).

Richter, Helmut, *Franz Kafka* (Berlin: Ruetten & Loening, 1962).

Robert, Marthe, *Seul, comme Franz Kafka* (Paris: Calmann-Levy, 1979).

Robertson, Ritchie, *Kafka: Judaism, Politics and Literature* (Oxford: Oxford University Press, 1985).

Sokel, Walter, *Franz Kafka: Tragik und Ironie* (Munich: Wels, 1964).

Speirs, Ronald, and Sandberg, Beatrice (eds.), *Franz Kafka* (London: Macmillan, 1997).

Stern, J. P. (ed.), *The World of Franz Kafka* (London: Thames & Hudson, 1980).

—— *The Heart of Europe* (Oxford: Blackwell, 1992).

—— *The Dear Purchase* (Cambridge: Cambridge University Press, 1995).

Sussman, Henry, *Franz Kafka: Geometrician of Metaphor* (Madison: Coda Press, 1979).

Thiher, Allen, *Franz Kafka: A Study of the Short Fiction* (Boston: Twayne, 1990).

Udoff, Alan (ed.), *Kafka and the Contemporary Critical Performance* (Bloomington, Ind.: Indiana University Press, 1987).

Wagenbach, Klaus, *Franz Kafka: Eine Biographie seiner Jugend* (Bern: Francke Verlag, 1958).

Zischler, Hanns, *Kafka geht ins Kino* (Reinbek bei Hamburg: Rowohlt, 1996).

Index